GALACTIC PILGRIM

GALACTIC PILGRIM

Poems by

Daniel Orsini

Quaternity™

GALACTIC PILGRIM

Quaternity Books™

Copyright © 2005 by Daniel Orsini

Third Edition Quaternity™ Books 2019

ISBN – 9781943691104

Cover Design by James Buchanan

*This book is dedicated to David Orsini, Daniel's twin brother—
an empathetic guide and a keen-sighted reader.*

"Do you understand all these things?" They answered, "Yes." And he replied, "Then every scribe who has been instructed in the kingdom of heaven is like the head of a household who brings from his storeroom both the new and the old."

~ Matthew 13.51-52

Permanence is but a word of degrees.

~ Ralph Waldo Emerson, "Circles"

CONTENTS

Preface	11	Heir Presumptive	42
Introduction	13	Heterotic	43
		Hourglass	44
Apostolates	19	An Image of an Image	45
Astronaut	20	Inmate of Space	46
Bio	21	In the Line of Melchizedek	47
Borderline Noun	22	Jack-o'-Lantern	48
Bowknot	23	Liquid Metal Man	49
The Cheshire of Sense	24	Living in Curved Space	50
Cinderdust	25	Navel	51
Citizen of the Cosmos	26	Orbifold	52
A Cloud in Slow Motion	27	Orpheus' Rite	53
Courtship	28	The Path of Least Action	54
The Crowned Hermaphrodite	29	The Power of Life	55
Crystal	30	The Quantum Alice	56
A Cup of Water	31	The Round Chaos	57
Elapid's Cowl	32	Saturn's Gramophone	58
The End of Ourselves	33	Servant of Nature	59
Entwining the Light	34	The Set-Up	60
Eros' Meal	35	Spacetime's Handkerchief	61
Finite Infinite	36	Spinner	62
The Foliate Pebble	37	Split-Minded	63
Galactic Pilgrim	38	Tabernacled	64
Gamonymous	39	Tattoo	65
God's Folly	40	Trismegistus' Art	66
God's Semaphore	41	Notes and Comments	67

PREFACE

These poems, which examine the spiritual as well as the psychological effects of being a Christian, offer an amalgam of diverse yet related influences: John Donne's "Holy Sonnets"; Alfred, Lord Tennyson's *In Memoriam A.H.H.*; and Emily Dickinson's "Behind me—dips Eternity—." Another significant source may also be apparent: the sonnet sequences of such Renaissance poets as Edmund Spenser, Sir Philip Sidney, and William Shakespeare. I must add, however, that, although the poems in this book generate a sense of thematic sequence, and although—composed of octets with variable rhyme schemes—they proceed in the same stanzaic form, they are, most decidedly, not sonnets. Rather, they are, as samples of formal poetry, what I prefer to call either "triads" (since each poem contains three stanzas) or "quaternals" (a coinage that underscores the role of the reader—not unlike that of the author—as the fourth component, the co-creative entity, that responds to, and intertwines with, each triadic structure). The "3 + 1" motif—the quaternity—is, as students of Jungian psychology may know, a spontaneous symbol of the self recognized in the figure of the crucified Christ, an archetype of wholeness that surfaces everywhere in *Galactic Pilgrim*.

Not surprisingly, then, these patterned lyrics seek to unfold—through form no less than through content—a unified and coherent *philosophic* vision steeped in the model life of the Christian Redeemer. In this regard, I would echo here a creative principle once expressed by Joseph Conrad, a statement of artistic purpose not unrelated to the aim implicit throughout *Galactic Pilgrim*: My business is to make you see; this is all, but that is everything.

Daniel Orsini

INTRODUCTION:
The Text of Our Faith
Daniel Orsini

"Whatever a man does in reality he himself becomes." To my mind, these words, written by C. G. Jung,[1] aptly define the spiritual trajectory of *Galactic Pilgrim*. Again and again, the poems of this book suggest that we enter the world at large in order to locate within ourselves the light that we perceive. Each of us being but a paraphrase of Adam and Eve, we walk upon Earth; leave our trace or footmark, so to speak; and then pass. Yet, wound in chaos though we are, Christ tabernacles us so that, without offense[2]—as He has told us—we may become apostles of His living Presence. Here and now, alert to His sufferings of light,[3] we may taste the "hidden manna," imagine our new names on the white stones that He shall assign to us (Rev. 2.17),[4] and know who we are. So Saint Paul, translating Our Savior's intent, has fittingly said: "I have been crucified with Christ: the life I now live is not my life, but the life which Christ lives in me [. . .]" (Gal. 2.20). As children of the light, we no doubt realize, when we meditate upon God's plan, that this is, of course, the same metamorphosis of which, momentarily trapped in his own void, Didymus dreamed: a religious conversion framed by history (John 20.24-29). Haltingly, humbly, *Galactic Pilgrim* takes as its subject, even as it witnesses, certain patterns of that sublime transformation.

Those patterns, often unbidden primordial images, derive, in my worldview, from the universal archetypes that Jung posits and that, everywhere, the Bible illustrates. In general, the poems collected in this volume underscore one basic belief, and it is this—that, Christ having entered the world, we may reclaim, through Him, the meaning of God's symbols. Indwelled and infilled by the Spirit of Christ, we can—palpably, in material forms, yet like breath bodies[5]—track both the outer and the inner darkness. Now, after Golgotha, not only can we explore the personal unconscious so that we may confront the Shadow, the proclivity to evil, that exists within each of us; we can also probe the collective unconscious so that we may assimilate, and indeed constellate, the divine contents—the spontaneous archetypes—that we discover there.

Clearly, throughout human history, such iconic models of the Absolute have nourished the Christian sojourner: the birth of Our Lord at Bethlehem, "the city of David" (Luke 2.1-20); His baptism "at Bethany on the banks of the Jordan" (Matt. 3.13-17); His temptation in "the wilderness" (Matt. 4.1-11); His transfiguration "on a high mountain" (Mark 9.2-8); His multiplication of the loaves at an unspecified "lonely place" (Matt. 14.13-21); His changing of the water into wine at Cana-in-Galilee (John 2.1-11); and then, later, His institution of the Eucharist during the Last Supper at Jerusalem (Luke 22.14-20); His crucifixion at Calvary (Matt. 27.32-54); His descent into Sheol, the place of the dead (Matt. 27.50-53); and, shortly thereafter, His appearances at the Sepulcher (John 20.11-18), on the road to Emmaus (Luke 24.13-35), and by the Sea of Tiberius (John 21.1-14). In the long run, all of these events—to many Christians, most cogent, perhaps, as still-evolving psychic situations, the lifeline of our liturgy—have proven advantageous to the species, mainly because they serve to canalize, creatively, the instinctual energy of both the individual and the group. Seemingly inherent in human nature, these fleshly symbols—inspiriting semaphores as much as they are analogues of salvation—prod us not only to "entwine" within ourselves the material rays of perception, but also to "testify" or "bear witness to" the "real light which enlightens every man" (John 1.7-9), that is to say, the cleansing light of redemption. In other words, having been "baptized into union with Christ Jesus" (Rom. 6.3), and hence nudged by the Holy Spirit, we see that we shall live again. This is the idea, the wavelength of clearsight[6] that Saint Paul punctuates further in Romans 6.4: "By baptism we were buried with him, and lay dead, in order that, as Christ was raised from the dead in the splendour of the Father, so also we might set our feet upon the new path of life."

Thus, the most significant of the archetypal structures listed above remains, as these poems indicate, the memorial of Christ's death and Resurrection—the Holy Eucharist itself. The very gist of this book is that, through Our Savior's self-sacrifice, and the salvation that He offers us, each believer, sharing in the ministry of Christ, is, or can be, "a priest for ever" according to the order of Melchizedek (Ps. 110.4). In effect, we concelebrate with Christ the perpetual (self-) sacrifice of the Mass, an unbloody rite steeped, paradoxically, in "the blood of the covenant" (Matt. 26.28). As Abraham the patriarch gave Melchizedek, "king of Salem" and "priest of God Most High, [. . .] a tithe of everything as his portion" (Heb. 7.1-2), so too we may surrender to God, not mere "spoil" (Heb. 7.4), but rather another form of wealth, Christ's living sacrifices, namely, His believer-priests. Indeed, as members of His Mystical Body, we can enter the sanctuary of Heaven, even now, through "the curtain [. . .] of His flesh" (Heb. 10.19-20). Moreover, because "we have been justified through faith" (Rom. 5.1), we can obtain spiritual as well as psychological wholeness if we but repeat within ourselves, as a daily mode of being, the salvific life and death of the Risen Jesus. Should the reader seek to chart the storyboard that links the forty-eight poems that span *Galactic Pilgrim*, he or she will find it precisely here—not in the braided plots of conventional (albeit pleasurable) fiction, but rather in the blissful transformations of our fallen humanity according to the Way of the Cross. I cannot emphasize this idea enough: Salvation through the Word of God—the determinate text of our faith—is conceived in this work, whether implicitly or explicitly, as the archetypal narrative of the Cross informed, and reified, by the spiritual experience at once common and unique to each individual.

Nevertheless, although I would italicize the Christological focus of these lyrics, I am not unaware of the ambiguities—philosophic no less than perceptual—that beset a Christian today. In fact, I have foregrounded the bittersweet dilemmas of our earthly fate amply throughout *Galactic Pilgrim*. As the offspring of a century mired in uncertainty, a contemporary Christian scribe who has been instructed "in the kingdom of Heaven" (Matt. 13.52) may not, I think, proceed otherwise. For, if, with every observation—as learned scientists have long since theorized—subject and object become indistinguishable as they interface, because one mirrors the other self-referentially; and, too, if this new concept of quantum identity riddles no less than subverts the idea of a unified and integrated self; and, further, if with its wavelike subatomic underpinnings macroscopic reality—or what we name macroscopic reality—splinters, at its core, the elusive coherence of the moment,[7] then morally, as heirs to His Kingdom (Jas. 2.5), we have no choice: Since everything that comes from God belongs to God (1 Chron. 29.11), we must acknowledge as frames of reference critical to the meaning of our lives—despite their jarring implications—all of God's mysteries.

    At the same time, however, having been incorporated into the pneumatic Christ through faith in Him, and therefore being "clothed with immortality" (1 Cor. 15.53), we need not jettison our dream of a holistic life. On the contrary, we can—even while this paradox of the finite infinite coils round us—kiss the snake that bites us, as it were, aware that, in any priestly text, the writer's utterance, being merely approximate, and the reader's grasp, being only selective, can lead the Christian wayfarer none the less not just to this earthly sphere of material knowledge, but to another place as well—in truth, to an Edenic realm of new revelation and new thought; that is to say, to such heavenly copy as Christ has drawn and shall, I believe, continue to draw from His tabernacled species. Simply enough, upraised as spiritual bodies (1 Cor. 15.44), we have "put on Christ as a garment" (Gal. 3.27). In effect, we "are all one person in Christ Jesus" (Gal. 3.28). For, as Jung himself reminds us, "'Jesus is still in the making.'"[8] Having become "a heavenly habitation" (2 Cor. 5.2) embodied by members of His "holy priesthood" (1 Pet. 2.5), Our Savior is now—and shall forever be—"a choice cornerstone" (1 Pet. 2.6), "the foundation-stone" (Eph. 2.20), "the keystone" (Acts 4.11), "a building which God has provided—a house not made by human hands" (2 Cor. 5.1), a "temple" (1 Cor. 3.16)—in fine, a "church" (Matt. 16.18) both mystical and fleshly to whose material altar we daily repair and to whose living Presence, I trust, these poems testify.

ENDNOTES

[1] Jung explores this theme in *Psychology and Alchemy*, trans. R. F. C. Hull (1952; Princeton: Princeton UP, 1980) 204.

[2] In *The Sickness unto Death*, trans. Alastair Hannay (1849; New York: Penguin, 1989), Søren Kierkegaard suggests that, as a sinner, the individual "is separated from God by the most yawning qualitative abyss" and that "God is separated [...] from man in turn by the same yawning qualitative abyss when he forgives sins" (155). Accordingly, from His bema-seat in Heaven, God *looks down*. Yet, strangely enough, through His unbridgeable distance, He empowers Christianity. Indeed, this *is* Christianity: "with this [stipulation] Christianity begins." It says to each particular human being: "either you shall be offended [because you shall be judged by the infinite Redeemer], or you shall believe. Not one word more; there is nothing more to add" (155-56).

[3] In *Catching the Light: The Entwined History of Light and Mind* (1993; New York: Oxford UP, 1995), Arthur Zajonc explains that "To know is to have seen, not passively but actively, through the action of the eye's fire, which reaches out to grasp, and so to apprehend the world" (22). In effect, "Sight entails the seer in an essential, formative action of image making or imagination." Significantly, Zajonc adds that, in the Christian worldview, "without [Christlike] trials of sacrifice and love, performed in utmost humility, the light of resurrection could not shine" (46).

[4] See *The New English Bible with the Apocrypha* (1961; New York: Oxford UP, 1972). Subsequent Biblical references are to this ecumenical text.

[5] In *Alchemical Studies*, trans. R. F. C. Hull (1967; Princeton: Princeton UP, 1983), C. G. Jung defines this ancient "psychic" concept as "a pneumatic body which is to serve us as a future dwelling, a body which, as Paul says, is put on like a garment [...]" (52). In other words, Christ indwells His believer-priest. As Andrew Murray reminds us in *The Spirit of Christ* (Pennsylvania: Whitaker House, n.d.): "Each of us must learn to know that there is a Holiest of All in that temple which we are" (210).

[6] See Zajonc 340: "every manifestation of light is potentially the occasion for the true grasping of light [...]. Each instance offers an occasion for enlightenment [...]," or clearsight.

[7] Gerald L. Schroeder ponders wave-particle duality and the "hybrid reality" that we inhabit in *The Science of God* (1997; New York: Broadway Books, 1998) 149-57.

[8] C. G. Jung cites this theological opinion in *Aion: Researches into the Phenomenology of the Self*, trans. R. F. C. Hull (1959; Princeton: Princeton UP, 1978) 221n157. The original source is R. Roberts, "Jesus or Christ?—A Reply," *The Quest*, vol. 2 (London, 1911) 124.

GALACTIC PILGRIM

APOSTOLATES

Like astronauts we offer God His clay;
Float in the chaos; that we may not stray,
To Spacetime tethered, skim the cargo bay;
Secure His unit; execute His play;
Suspend His coheir even as we pray
That, children of the sun, we track His ray;
With semaphores Our Savior show the way;
Gethsemane once more restore the day.

Round as a chasuble, Spirit swaggers,
Upraises His staff; His *rebis* staggers,
Calls to His site both pacers and laggers,
Pierces the void, its swath but a dagger's.
White as solid snow He flies in the storm.
Apostolates of colors shall He form:
Ge's elevated Host, its foreparts warm,
Inside the lion's carcass combs that swarm.

I know a man *that* intimate with dust
He forecasts from his scaffold winds that gust;
Measures his monarch, foetus like a crust;
Ingests His substance, wafer since he must.
So everyone may taste eternal life:
His sacerdotal feast, its altars rife.
Dear to Him as Isaac, curved as a knife,
Christ's believer-priest is sealed as a wife.

ASTRONAUT

Whereas the toad submersed in solid earth
Awaits its house to compensate its berth,
The heron borne on air abrim with sun
Receives in its eyes its rays like a nun.
And still the shaman reenacts the feat:
Stag and unicorn in the forest meet.
His cross-beam, hoisted, quarters like a clock;
His Psyche, splintered, pantomimes Her shock.

Figures yet arise: the ring in the well,
Cloudform that rouses, coalfish in the swell,
Serpent in the garden, Adam in its spell,
Predestinate the Savior in His shell:
Hermaphrodite echoic as a bell,
Clapper in the fracas, measure in the knell,
Above, Below, both Up and Down that mell
In hyperspace or God's Edenic dell.

Wrapped in gossamer, crosshatched strips that furl,
Snowy quintessence, torso bands that burl,
My rugged suit somatic in the swirl,
Near my right elbow tether hooks that curl,
I walk upon the moon as round as glass;
Craters everywhere, rock chips that I class,
I stake my stiffened banner, shift my mass,
Implant my furrowed print, and then I pass.

BIO

Above the sift of mud and sand like slate,
Cephalopod mollusks in forms that date;
Crinoids, bryozoans, starfish that bait;
Fossil coelacanths, scales that imbricate
Before the teleosts, Devonian freight:
Corals, trilobites, hyoliths—*that* late,
Triassic sponges, limestone from the plate,
Hominid skeletons, bones such as mate.

Noctuids in amber, chafers that fly,
Hoofed mammals, primates, the makers of *pi*—
How every atom, concretized, taunts me!
And still one other; phantom it haunts me:
In pools of light we shall sit in a ring
In cloth-of-gold robes, both coheir and King,
In patterns older than our piety,
Hyaline circling all society.

Eve's son and Adam's, tertiary key,
Integral relative from Jesse's tree.
With this I conclude my biography.
And if any question my ancestry...?
Say then that I woke outside the palace,
The wound on the planet: nub or callus,
Shaman, *soror*, mandrake in the chalice,
Christ astride the chaos with His ballasts.

BORDERLINE NOUN

We are His issue, offspring of the spoil,
In the pelican such molecules as roil,
Seed in the residue, sown men that moil,
Paraphrase of Adam cooked to a boil,
Red Damascene earth upraised from its coil.
At the rim of the cluster, spinners toil:
Leaf in the litter, scarab in the soil,
Orb-web's crucifer, Ouroboros' foil.

I drew the specter out of the vessel;
Dispersed its flesh with mortar and pestle;
His Son contiguous, thus would nestle;
With that archetype years did I wrestle.
Ejected from Eden, wound in the void,
Nebo receding, by cloudforms convoyed,
I strode the cosmos; my spacesuit yet buoyed,
Assumed His staff, the God with Whom I toyed.

A city like a crystal, End-time's town,
The Self is a clock that never runs down.
Awash in glass, its mass both light and brown,
I trace a face that in the font may drown:
Galactic gargoyle, interstellar clown,
Regurgitated bubble, death mask's frown,
Gethsemane's coheir, Calvary's crown,
Conjugated verb-stem, borderline noun.

BOWKNOT

What do men desire after Martian rock?
The instant of lift-off, a drogue to dock,
A cinctured suit to rove the chaos, stock
Astride the moon some transcendental clock.
Gamonymous Ge in veils that He loathes
Undrapes Herself, disperses all Her clothes,
Denounces Her familiar Time with oaths,
Then carries Him, the ghost that She betroths.

This world is, say, Her bowknot, gyve or bind;
A loop recursive, self-excited, blind;
A line of scarlet; Eve with Adam twined;
A piece of string that round the mind can wind.
He raises us till on a cloud we change;
A stretch of time He generates our range;
Metabolized in us, both seed and grange,
He stands without a skein, transparent, strange.

We reconnoiter, shuttle to the sun
That we may see His face; the Father done,
Abraham, the Paraclete, Mary's nun—
Every atom spun on Möbius' run.
A pinpoint of light; primordial broth;
The essence of the cosmos: layered froth;
The fingered Jesus, seamless like a cloth,
Like a peacock studded, folded like a moth.

THE CHESHIRE OF SENSE

From point to pyre: the static in the horn;
Shadow matter; parallel Flatland shorn;
Upon the tree the scattered sun disk torn
Like flakes of fire; the foetus not yet born.
All round us in sections remnants of night:
Sepia threshold; lammergeier's wight:
The Infant candled; Anna at the rite,
The Savior dandled—sundered from all sight.

Constrained as Moses, manna on his tooth,
He sits like a shade, a man in his booth
Alert to the noise, transparent as truth
Some distant antiphon grasped in his youth:
Noctuid moths that infiltrate the porch.
Their gossamer wings yet flap in the torch
Like Echo's orisons, embers that scorch,
Listless millipedes that click in the watch.

Like us He ascends, in such dust as dents—
Rotund alembic, void that circumvents
Turbid residue—takes us to His tents
Outside Spacetime; *Heaven's Cheshire of sense*,
He fades from insight, Nature's recompense:
Tethered the unit—minuscule, immense—
That on the chaos stands, maneuvers hence,
Then nears His bema seat without offense.

CINDERDUST

Conglomerate God, His Sonship threefold—
Archon's soma, Gaea's cauldron keyholed,
Archon's pneuma—synthesized His freehold
That we may bear His substance, as He told:
Carnal as the cross where His bone must knit,
Leprous as the moon where His soul shall sit,
Subtile as the sun where His ghost has lit
Sundered from all secondness, whole or slit.

Chosen by God as in the beginning,
Disks like dross throughout the chaos spinning,
Same faint static in the psyche dinning
Past Creation, Yahweh's Cheshire grinning,
We roll the ball as into a sinter;
Experience space, abyss like winter;
Test the celerity of the sprinter;
Rub away the pupil, beam not splinter.

I pray for wings that I may not sink down.
My unit white, Her crystal throne earth-brown,
I skim its sphere transparent as a noun,
Like Jesus self-related. Spirit's crown,
He vitrifies my helmet, suits my clown,
Invests my astronaut, His marble gown
Like ash or cinderdust or any down
That, biform, capsules me or star or town.

CITIZEN OF THE COSMOS

At Spacetime's junction, when all was ready
And starlight trickled into the eddy,
By spring-point of Pisces, goat or teddy—
According to theory, swing or steady—
This molecule arose, and then said He
Such bread as He had wed, and then led He
These dead to His spread, a water shed He,
And at His head we fed, and then sped He.

And still His motion bubbles in the broth:
Void like the adder, shadow like the Goth,
Web like the whirlwind, every specter wroth
Until the foam unfurls and then a froth,
A lace and then a face and then a moth
And then His star man laid as on a swath,
Gamonymous His side and then a cloth,
Synonymous His bride and then a troth.

Resident of the planet, atoms massed,
Genus authenticated, species classed,
Gender instantiated, spouses fast,
Migrant yet hyphenated, unit glassed,
We extricate the Aeon from the past,
Galeate the Savior, wound in the cast—
Citizen of the cosmos born at last—
Embrace Him in the trace, both small and vast.

A CLOUD IN SLOW MOTION

As if I had swung from atom to wave
Or flung in the void or hung in the nave,
I stiffed like a moth till one sent to save
Had poured His elixir that He might lave
My sutured astronaut. Then had His knave
Wound me in chaos like Adam, Eve's slave,
Joseph in the cistern, Christ in His cave.
But what was I doing out of *my* grave?

Since life and death like spouses intertwine,
Cloud-borne the body—both wafer and wine,
His *crowned hermaphrodite*—transcends its spine.
We pass at climax through the thinnest line.
I cannot say that Jesus did not say
What it means to drop or dangle at play
Or thrust from Flatland feel the scaffold sway
Or climb down space or pray the unit stay.

Astride the chaos self-propelled we join
A perfect circle even as a coin
Seamless on its track may, stochastic, wind.
Flight's trajectory, it stirs in my mind
A cloud in slow motion, wave on the shore
That streaks like a web, a stone at its core.
Tabernacled now I enter its door
Without offense. I have been here before.

COURTSHIP

In Gaea's house, where Unity once knocked,
We try each door that the Hubble unlocked:
Coal Sack and Cepheid, Cloverleaf clocked,
Like Centaurus A, by its dust ring blocked.
Ancient as a sage, a photon can fly
Across the aeons; the retina ply,
Encased in parsecs, Ge's numinous spy:
The spagyric foetus coiled in its eye.

We have trampled on the garment of shame;
Aberrant as matter, assign the blame;
Exalted at last by Hosea's claim,
Neither male nor female nor *rebis* name.
By beasts, and birds, and things that creep perplexed,
We script such a text as Ge has annexed—
Some sapphirine premise; no longer vexed,
The map of Her body, our muscles flexed.

When old stars in globular clusters merge,
Out of their ashes protoplanets surge
Even as particles that spheroids urge
Outside the horizon or, inside, purge.
Still galaxies slide or mix in the light,
As Hermes observes; to his smitten sight,
Courtship in the cosmos the strangest rite.
Like us he is not alone in the night.

THE CROWNED HERMAPHRODITE

Rotund as Adam, steward of the bee
Unequal with God, yet a form of Ge,
A man is but twofold, woman the key,
The true star in him Eve's Rabbinic tree.
Cimmerian Maya, vault of the sea,
Cloister, crypt, or cave, She twines by decree
Temenos or tee, the cleft that we flee,
That we may rise in loving bondage free.

His wand like a circlet, hook like a mace,
Ring like a cincture, torso like a brace;
The root of all, his *rebis*, but the trace
Of Jesus' horn, lamellicorn its base,
He navigates the void without a face:
Atman, manikin—bound by Clotho's lace
Astride the globe, his unit yet apace—
The crowned hermaphrodite encased by space.

An astronaut is an uncommon man.
Ensconced in his craft, he orbits its span;
Glides above the disk; at length in his van,
Conjoins his cyborg; in layers that scan,
Untethered in Spacetime, thrusts where he can;
Shuttlewalks the dark; then, sealed by its ban—
Scion like a bubble, mote like a clan,
Tribe like a beam—begins where he began.

CRYSTAL

Equipped with sensors, Kevlar chassis, thighs
Immersed in matter, astronaut that hies
In tumult or terror, body that plies
By Jesus salted, extract of the wise,
I rove the funnelweb; scaffold the skies;
Accost the tesseract; target the prize;
Hyacinthine light akin to my size,
In the cubic form of a crystal, rise.

Conglomerate soul, assembly of whims,
Bird of Hermes, preexistent He brims.
Like foam in the cavern, subset that swims:
Some fractal in the mind, or silent hymns,
He fashions the shaman: foot that He trims,
Flock of His pasture: remnant that He skims,
This blessed greenness: agate that He dims,
And I am His sparks, and I am His limbs.

When Gaea tends Her garden, dressed in white,
Convalescent heart, She sections the blight;
With even the ruthlessness of the kite,
Transplants the sun and then nurtures the night:
Rust of the metals; Adam Kadmon's rite:
Rubeous foetus; in the leprous light,
Till all of the souls shall have left his sight,
Pale blue sapphire of the hermaphrodite.

A CUP OF WATER

Matter wars in us, Yahweh having lent,
From Eden, Gaea's simple; Heaven rent,
Antinomies of scent; what Adam meant
When he mounted Eve: the residue blent.
We squander the absolute in the fact;
Reality's integral in the act:
Diaphany stretched, entelechy sacked,
Totality sundered, Salvation wracked.

We reach inside the skull a zone of power;
Round us wrap its cortices; like a bower,
Resorb the Euphrates; spark like a shower,
Seize the distillate that falls from the flower;
Regard *the goose of Hermes* as a dower,
The body of our wisdom; vas or tower,
Assimilate the contents: dipper, plower,
The stone that has a spirit, Jew or Giaour.

He was the tree stump; ringed at length in years,
Had quartered Spacetime; with His pair of shears,
Cut the line of Clotho; lassoed His steers;
Vented Hecate's cauldron; shifting His gears,
Maneuvered His unit; hosted His doom;
Dispersed His phantom; garment on the loom,
Upraised His urn; rotundum like a groom,
Set down His cup . . . *there* . . . and then left the room.

ELAPID'S COWL

As I shift the blind, I ignore the spurge.
For there, where Belvedere and Sachem urge
Conjunction at my lot if not a surge
Within the precinct, path and sky converge.
And then I greet the Cheshire in the street,
Raccoon by the oak, some loller in heat,
Till I scan where he ran: his sprinter's cleat,
Upon the peat, a boson like a beat.

Strewn scintillae, paraselenae sped,
Elapid's cowl, inside the human head
Eve's gamonymus, manna that He spread,
With *this* left over, as the Lord has said.
Hangdog, without excuse, since Satan strayed,
Numbered are we, inmate, measured and weighed
Even as a shade, the Noun that He bade,
Leaf veins that deliquesce, crown that we braid.

A bearded beehive, a hooded hollow,
The queen departs, and death-duels follow.
At the nuptial flight, their remnants earth-brown,
In motion like sections, embers tamped down,
Cabiri yet burn, then spurn their metals.
Verdigris essential, twilight kettles
While I at my tripod time-lapse the day.
Bulky cumuli boil across the bay.

THE END OF OURSELVES

I am that alien, goatfoot with horn
Engendered by the cosmos; foetus born
As faint as a triangle: Capricorn;
Like Sirius rising, Orion worn
Even as a belt, or Omphale's thorn,
Infected I became, a boy forlorn;
Perfected twice a girl; immune to scorn,
Eve's imprint from the heart of matter torn.

How do we come to the end of ourselves?
This nature that conquers the natures delves
Till it races to grace; upon its shelves
Sets its Cabir; oracular as elves
Ascends to the top of the retort, selves
Probabilistic, selfsame quantum selves,
The three times the four, continuous selves
Everywhere spinning, like Maria's twelves.

Coheir I shall see when I scale the peak
Sapientia in Her solar teak;
Son of the Father, miter like a beak,
The bema-seat Jesus, King that I seek,
Smitten, round, galactic; spouses *that* sleek,
Galeated offspring, emulous clique;
Soul like a crystal, Spirit like a streak—
Like Solomon himself, I cannot speak.

ENTWINING THE LIGHT

Unseen from the womb, *unshod and unarmed*,
I squint at the tint; if, by candles charmed,
Should husk the dusk...? Some phantom, more alarmed,
Might doubt my witness, day's own image harmed
Less by ghouls than by idolatry's schools.
Light, being malleable, plies his tools
With rivets of love till hung as on spools
The Son entwines the sun, and the Son rules.

Let the clock stall and hand fall and time end;
Each automaton, sight's Pandora, wend
Purblind its way; like discards, comets spend;
Galactic clusters that shun us distend;
Cyborgs yet scout the vacuum and rend,
And matter bend, and pictures all upend—
Hephaestus, the nets of Atropos pend:
To know is to see, to see but to blend.

Suspect meson, quotidian decay;
Quark and anti-quark; wavelength like a ray—
What then is life? Among Jehovah's homes,
A cornucopia of chromosomes;
Webwork of tissue: foetus in its sac;
Cast out an error: atom on the rack;
Sod that instructs: rotundum in its blouse,
God that tucks in the cosmos of His spouse.

EROS' MEAL

As even the god entwined in its lobe,
Complete, illumined, purged, we span the globe.
Sirius, Procyon, star like a strobe—
Canopus' copy: unit, ghost or probe.
In the googolsphere such photons as flee
Can, in the soul, hierarchical, see:
Mary with her moon-eye, vine like a tree,
Shroud like a hood, as hierodules decree.

Bulbous as an hourglass, infinite eight,
Curved as a cincture, buxom as a mate,
Round as a lasso, Ouroboros' bait,
Hermes slips through the narrow soon or late.
To cultivate the high I seized the sky,
To calculate the lie thus eased the guy,
To consummate His sigh appeased the tie,
Half teased the die in the pit of my eye.

We are without excuse things that are made:
Seahorse, ammonite, colubrid that braid,
Curlicue acacia, quail that He bade,
Cobwebby hoarfrost, such dew as He laid.
This is Eros' meal: It need not be doled.
Feast of Aphrodite, cauldron all gold
Fastened with rivets, the eyeball is bold.
The story of light has yet to be told.

FINITE INFINITE

We scan like mist or cloud across the sky
Nebulae patent to an avid eye,
Ponder ephemerides on a map,
Then feed hypnotic from our mother's lap:
Yoke like a harrow's, horn in the Sahel,
Heaven's chasuble buxom as a bell,
Bead in the basalt, point or serpent knit,
Creed of the tortoise: finite infinite.

Children of the cosmos, risen, zealous,
These are the signs if any can quell us,
As if we awoke, confronted Tellus,
Ishtar or parallel Ge in Hellas,
Then shared Her secret, Mary's adept terse:
Every Great Mother constellates a nurse,
Nourishes the raven, atoms converse,
The Paraclete steers, and we marry the hearse.

Reckless I entered the world through a crack;
Propelled my unit; restive in the sac—
Eyeslit or demon, pebble that you thwack—
Twined my umbilical; rabid to pack,
In sections maneuvered him; stack on stack,
Delivered him to Zion; Spacetime black,
Flung high the capsule; hung as on a rack,
To nothingness nailed him on Yahweh's track.

THE FOLIATE PEBBLE

Vega passing, Arcturus like a crust,
Pinwheel astronaut, I peer through the dust:
Shell like a nautilus; spool like a gust
That curves round itself as a foetus must;
Ring like the sun-disk; moonbeam in the rust;
Tailspun like a serpent, nematode trussed—
Crescent self-sown; out of Reason or Lust,
Foliate pebble into Sheol thrust.

Antinomy's light, cosmogony's hum,
Sphere of the Trinity He is the sum:
Rivers of water, belly that we plumb
Centered as we spiral, coitus' gum.
Resin of the wise concealed in the drum
Even as Christ, particulate or crumb;
Like Mars and Venus, concrete as a thumb,
Embodied the door, emboldened we come.

Coheir of the Kingdom, ribboned aster,
Cinctured Asclepius, adept pastor,
Root of itself, hyacinthine master,
The One, the All, in the fissure vaster,
I stood on the chaos; reeled out past her;
Imprint of the Spirit, heart's pilaster,
Temple of Maya, held my prey faster.
Some doors open from the inside, Castor.

GALACTIC PILGRIM

A singularity is but a point,
The body moribund that we anoint,
Unshelled in the crescendo, out of joint
The Spirit vanishing till He appoint
Transparencies in Spacetime, such a snow
As cloudform, swan, or solar wheel may sow,
Or moonplant in the vas, or in the flow
His tethered unit, target of the bow.

As steep in the fissure shadows rattle,
Upon the altar scimitars tattle,
Or tumbles the infant till hands that hoist
Release enfleshed His ghost without a joist,
In the berm by the creek the lizard strays;
Round the herm in the garden flowers like rays,
In beds of humus couched, suborn the worm,
Entwine the crossbar, vindicate the term.

Jack-o'-lantern winked out, Cheshire that rare,
Silken funnelweb dangled by a hair;
The thief beside Him, Christ inside its snare,
Hierophant at sunrise astride His mare.
Still the trumpeter orchestrates His blare.
Galactic pilgrim, meditate His flare:
Ge's hyphenate gamonymous and fair,
Everyone is on his way to somewhere.

GAMONYMOUS

I scale His tesseract, salivate, nod,
Count as a virtue aromatic cod,
Saltpoint, pomegranate, wheat that we prod,
A twig in the retort; stone in the sod,
Crave but earthly substance—seed in the pod,
Peacemaker, *rebis*, shepherd with His rod,
Bema-seat Jesus, same biped that trod,
Slave to humankind, and witness to God.

We repent of our sin; believe into Christ;
Illumined thus, transform; each sense enticed,
Spirit, soul, and body having been spliced,
His vessel glorified, cleft that we priced,
Excise the suture; fertilize the strife;
Shunt the Savior's blood; maneuver the knife;
Serpent like a fife, elicit the life;
Entelechies rife, contract like a wife.

Wholeness canalized deep inside the skin,
The Queen at Her bowl, the King shut tight in,
Some specter enters matter that slumbers;
Aroused, redeemed, etheric as numbers,
Transmutes its substance; couples Space and Time;
Enshrines, gamonymous, coheirs that climb
Between His trees, till bride and groom that mount
Ply philosophy on their own account.

GOD'S FOLLY

When Jesus died, they dressed Him like a tot;
Swathed His cadaver; sealed Him in a grot;
Exhumed His Spirit; cooked Him in a pot;
Unloosed His foetus; swirl inside the clot,
Calcined His bones; released Him to a plot
Akin to Golgotha; midmost the spot,
Distilled His Host; His specter polyglot,
Frankincense scattered, houseled then His dot.

The world evolved as from a ghostly point;
Extended its corpse; connected each joint;
Its skeleton attached, its features coined,
Imparted such a dust as Ge conjoined.
Remnant of its coupling, root of its spawn,
An infant grew at length like cosmic dawn:
Embosomed *rebis*, victim round with brawn
Sprung from out Her tree like a statue sawn.

I riffle through Eve's physics in my den.
Human mysteries lie beyond my ken.
Still am I here; until I blink again,
Collapse the puzzle; whether now or then,
Reclaim God's archetype; like cock and hen,
Mind His commandment; apprehend His fen;
Marry the goatfoot that leaps from my pen.
Even God's folly proves wiser than men.

GOD'S SEMAPHORE

We learn through what happens; lexies indexed,
In real time, from one side to the next,
Unroll His scroll; the multiverse annexed,
Uprear such a sphere as Lucifer hexed:
Venus' downy myrtle, pelican vexed,
The same orbweb strewn before Adam, sexed,
Had twined its skein; inhabited the text;
Then mounted his tree-cross, Eve's biceps flexed.

A lizard wizard He blent with His doom;
Deepened Genesis; chaos with a boom,
Frolicked in its fire; sorrowed in its gloom;
Writhed in His garment on Lachesis' loom;
Made of Gethsemane His cosmic room;
Then raised each remnant: foetus in the womb,
Mary's sequoia, Eve's composite groom,
Yahweh's semaphore eyeballed at the tomb.

Exemplar of signs He pointed the way;
Threaded the cavern; having joined its clay,
Integrated thus, anointed His ray
That, however we coined it, dawn or day,
Even as we housed Him, beam on a tray,
Inside the chalice, or pyx since we may,
The Son might enter; see us at our play;
His tendrils pending, scale the cargo bay.

HEIR PRESUMPTIVE

Resurrection happens when we are born—
Bow in the cloud or foetus in the horn;
Zodiacal light, indistinct, forlorn,
That ancient Gate of Heaven: Capricorn,
The faintest triangle, Sol's sea goat worn;
Some Cheshire in the sky, its whiskers shorn;
Or elsewhen aswirl, its crucifer torn,
Same syzygy forsworn that long we mourn.

As if the Savior's glaive had swung my way,
And on its cusp I curved, or on His tray
I vacillated even as that stray,
The phantom in the vault, or night and day
That yet interfere, or Son, if I may,
Strapped to His pendulum, His mote at play,
I entered the void; descended like clay;
Baptized then, vitrified: His cinctured ray.

As offspring the Father, Father the Son;
Like Jesus' Mother, Eva's second, spun;
Housel plus the moon, a Trinity of One,
His heir presumptive I carry the sun,
Enfold His body, consecrate its sign,
Absorb the wafer, apprehend the wine,
Imagine each thorn that studded the vine—
Inmate of Earth, upon His altar dine.

HEROTIC

From a cloud we rise, a watery ring;
Descend like a stone; arrive like a king;
Immerse the subject, pebble in a spring;
Project the Savior, slipknot like a sling.
For birth on Earth is always happening.
The Acorn Barnacle yet rides its swing;
Slipper Limpets settle; seahorses cling:
Broken symmetries, heterotic string.

What matters is that it happen in me,
Sweet, unspotted, sated virginity.
Gabriel vouchsafing "Ave Mary,"
God seeded Her soul; its orbweb hairy,
Conquered Gehenna; recompense or wraith,
Had hurdled at once Her household of faith;
Set upon Her head a vine like a gourd;
Replenished Her Tree, the hoard of the Lord.

His visage in limestone, dust that he apes,
He lifts like a tool a strigil that scrapes;
Catalog of cultures, His warriors traipse;
Mirror of Ares, colonized, He gapes.
Aphrodite standing, avid She quests;
Inscrutable turban, tilted, She tests;
Terracotta priest, oracular, crests;
Foam like the cosmos, seals His salted breasts.

HOURGLASS

Every particle set, the cosmos swayed.
It was not a slight percept that I weighed:
Orbweb or sheetweb, snare that I had laid,
Nor string to the Kingdom: Phaëthon's braid—
Cloud upon cloudform; in my mind a shade,
His dusky image: Self upon the grade;
Against my rib cage anguish like a blade,
Till, through that cascade, God had made His raid.

The Great Chain stretches, iridescent band:
Moses, Elias, Yahweh's peacock fanned;
Simon's canopy, *three times four* trepanned.
Composite still, within this scheme I stand.
Plosive cumuli: what the eye had scanned;
Stricken integer: what the mind had spanned;
Parallel shaman: what the Ghost had planned;
Patterned sonship: Christ on Möbius' strand.

A content perceived by an observer,
Bulbous hourglass, however He curve her,
Random, existent, always with fervor,
Outside or inside, housels its server
Like Eden's symbols: polymorphous light,
Undivided point, both daystar and night,
Matrix of the Aeons, shepherd of the white,
Biform astronaut, Cross, hermaphrodite.

AN IMAGE OF AN IMAGE

The wheel upon my car had swung away,
Upheaved as with a thwack my finished clay,
Then ricocheted. I swear I heard it shear
Even as a blade the shade of my fear.
We know the world when it is tangible.
The tread *before* the spin, though frangible,
Flailed in the mud, and then the iron swam
On a borrowed stick. I am, *that* I am.

His body leonine, first Adam's form,
His spirit reconnoiters in the storm
Like bees that scale His comb. A ghostly swarm,
They tease their waxen selves; when it is warm,
Smear their silver dust, then lift from the pod
Hairy entelechies, like mammals shod,
Their essence—tabernacled: coil or rod—
Still an image of an image of God.

She washed His feet until her soul was clean,
Then kissed the Lord. His substance epicene,
A scarab self-born, He basked in His sheen;
Aroused the lame; increased the jar; serene,
Consoled the waters; healed the blind; when seen,
Upraised the Host; then, hyphenate His screen,
Beyond the globe, behind the void, between
Space and His trace, did housel what I mean.

INMATE OF SPACE

The world that we know is passing away:
Strange luminescences, traces of day,
Arms of plankton blooms, ships' wakes in the bay,
Parallel sand dunes, Horeb like a clay,
Footmark, leaf, nor lizard—these shall not stay—
Hill of Moriah, nor Hecate's stray:
Cheshire like the planet blue, white and gray;
Rabid the Dog Star that yet shows the way.

Vanishing the sun that both is and was,
As sealed as Moses or that man at Uz,
Secretes his liquid, deposits his fuzz,
Extrudes his trip lines as a trapdoor does.
Till one is born again, he may not see,
Conceived as in a capsule cannot flee,
Safe in his cubicle floats in the sea,
Then stands upon the globe by God's decree.

Entelechy's particle, solar calèche,
Bread in the chalice for the first time fresh,
He enters His Kingdom through web or mesh,
Veil or curtain *by the way of His flesh*;
Image tabernacled, ghost like a face,
Suspends in cloud, then roves without a trace:
Rebis that shapely, dyad in its case:
Skein of the Shekinah, inmate of space.

IN THE LINE OF MELCHIZEDEK

Lace like a lattice's, wheel like a scroll's,
Cosmos like a coal's, we transit His wolds;
Earth on its axis, sky on its poles,
Ascend Ge's horizon; zenith that holds,
Compose then like matter quicksilver molds:
Both round as a soul's and square as a knoll's—
Even as the Savior's, tense as a bole's—
The scaly webwork of the creature's folds.

At history's climax small as a bean,
Curled like a skein in my father's demesne,
Adam's crystalline bride—Eve's child, I mean:
Hyphenate wean—through the slit in the screen,
With water, marjoram, wool aubergine,
I washed in the flow of the Nazarene:
Ashes of the heifer, blood off the peen,
Then a high deep blue that He mixed with green.

He bound him to a spit; the altar razed,
Calcined him over stone; the shaman braised,
Like pottage from Edom the vessel crazed,
Vitrified his substance: utterance phrased.
Hierophant bucketed, Didymus dazed;
Astronaut braceleted, Cherubim grazed;
Coheir helmeted, Melchizedek praised:
Same priest as Jesus to His dais raised.

JACK-O'-LANTERN

Maya like the moon can juggle Her pins;
Pile around Her prey conglomerate skins;
Scale the winds; upon Leviathan's fins,
Solicit from the deep or store in tins
Transmundane matter, *Savior of the twins.*
And the phantom through the cochlea spins,
Same ancient light in the tympanum dins,
Inside my eye the jack-o'-lantern grins.

A man is but a cipher deified,
Woman still a bone picked out of his side,
Unless each apprehend that He did ride
Upon the waters; in the vessel bide;
Had on His pathway sacerdotal dried
The victim at the rack before He died;
Then, Bethany before them, blessed His bride,
Apostles of His presence reified.

The Self is—what?—some vas that Eros lent,
Siphon of a sort, the pelican sent
When the cloud subsides, and the pleasure spent
We ask the shaman what the treasure meant.
And if the static answer, Cheshire slink,
This strange acoustics pitch us to the brink . . . ?
Then stand on the chaos, swirl toward the sink,
Dispart the galaxy, and do not blink.

LIQUID METAL MAN

I run my race; at every thunderclap,
My body like the Cheshire's, close the gap,
Then stanch the flow, on hillside, track, or lap
All Heaven but a readout like a map,
Some hypsometric atlas, such a tint
As salves my eye when streaked by light I sprint,
Like metal glint, or coated as I squint
Do my stint, then harbor Septuagint.

Pinned down, plantigrade, determined to soar,
I reach His tabernacle; nudge its door;
Enter the universe; without a floor,
Dangle in space; like the funnelweb store
As in a sheet of silk; entangle; pore;
Upon such a cerecloth as Jesus wore—
Bunting smoother than linen—nibble, then bore,
Partake of my prey to His ghostly core.

I track a figure, phantom like a bole
Toward which I ascend, a foal, then a mole,
Some Maya that spins to Polestar or soul
Her skyey scroll. I navigate His knoll.
Truth is splintered: Mephistopheles' pup;
Hourglass yet sutured; flesh on which we sup;
Coheir smitten; hierophant like a cup;
Commingled spouse and housel, *right side up.*

LIVING IN CURVED SPACE

In Spacetime, after Yahweh sends the rain;
Encapsules Jesus' atom; like a grain
To Sheol hurtles Him; upon His wain,
He cinctures like a serpent Mary's brain;
At Skull Place savors Her; where He has lain,
Apperceives Her presence: Golgotha's swain.
Glass and the twain, substantiated, slain,
Hover and haver, suspended in pain.

I rise as I began; not yet a man,
Paraphrase the hyphenate; the woman plan;
Heaven to Earth, then Earth to Heaven fan;
Lift out of my side such skein as He ran:
Rumor of Rhea, patent in the scan;
Celestial utterance, point that I span;
Coheir, *rebis*, bride of His royal ban,
Teleport Ge's retort in Castor's van.

The world is like a string: It winds and winds
Even as the finger, spun from it, twines.
Crowned Ouroboros, sutured thus he dines;
Devours the cosmos; incubates; divines;
Like Mars and Venus implicated, grinds;
Re-collects the torus; coil that He binds,
Describes the center; strand that Ge enshrines,
Turns like a city in this band of lines.

NAVEL

Seek the dragon, Son of the sun by day,
Or Corascene, another kind of stray.
So moonwise you shall sit, yet cannot stay.
If you miss a turn you may lose the way.
Spacetime is steep, incisive as a swath,
Toroidal as foam, insistent as wrath.
Terse, abstruse, hyacinthine as a bath,
Step out in the light cone onto the path.

We twine the pine-tree; finger in the side,
Stand on the chaos; crowned like Jesus, stride.
Galactic coheirs, astronauts that ride
Espoused at the Sabbath, bema-seat bride—
These are such photons as hierophants paint.
We cross ourselves lest proximity taint.
And still we witness Him till biform, faint,
Rotund we steer His spacesuit like a saint.

Cursed at first we thirst till, being submersed,
Nursed in metallic waters, reimbursed,
The Host rehearsed, a wavier Savior pursed,
The world reversed, at length we are dispersed.
A moonship, a flow, a sapphirine snow,
A glow so slow that wherever we row
Or shrouded stow we grow before we show,
And then we know: Across the Styx we go.

ORBIFOLD

Heaven's vacuum: bubble like an ink.
He leans; aligns His hand; then, with each chink,
Adam pulverized, cleaves him at the brink.
Starry creation, Yahweh at the sink.
Fade to hyperspace, Quaternity's rink;
Some vibrating resonance like a kink:
Torus, orbifold, tunnel, Zion's link.
From Paradise stem all such forms as slink.

Line of Ouroboros, substance we dine
Even as his serpent: coil like a bine;
Euphrates' water; ladder of the vine;
Like Moses' God the adder in its spine,
The cloven pine. His Father's "branch of Mine"
Like Being beingless, sundered His shrine,
He is the door—there is no other sign.
I race His twine to the end of the line.

Devoid of content Spacetime is unknown:
Curvature in the sheet; the species sown,
Lace like a lattice; draped around His bone,
Garment from Edom; chiseled on His stone—
The whitest pebble—hypercube or cone,
Infinite assemblage, clone after clone
Contained within Her Son; the Savior prone,
The regimen of Mars in Venus' zone.

ORPHEUS' RITE

Galaxies that cluster, stars that arise,
Those that muster, some that cannibalize,
Hub like a trapdoor, satellite that spies,
Moonplant or hawkmoth, astronaut that hies:
The body, sensate, tabulates its size.
Seahorse that shudders, tawny owl that cries,
Quill worm that tunnels, razor shell that pries,
Raft snail that bubbles, stone that heated dries.

Idaean dactyl, ithyphallic wight,
Goblin, pixie, *puer*, thumbling *that* slight,
Triadic clay we circumcise the light,
Exhume from its tomb the maw of the mite,
The jaw of the bight, the caw of the kite,
Consecrate pleasure by an appetite.
Sunbeam at the window, hoofmark by night,
Ephesus' ritual, Orpheus' rite.

We enter the world as we might a spa,
From amniotic waters holler wa,
Sense diminution, burble da or ma,
Motion the Father: Brahma, Yahweh, Ra.
Encased diaphany, encapsuled ba,
Hyacinthine infant, embodied ka,
Tossed veronica, courtship's la-di-da,
Sigh crucifixal, copulative Ah.

THE PATH OF LEAST ACTION

Brethren, we see with the eyes of the heart:
Vestiges, images, hierophant's art,
Primordial atoms that ravel smart,
Cluster galaxies that satellites chart.
And still the cosmos hangs upon its hook.
In the icy light we squint and then look.
Spacetime's Leviathan, beak of a rook,
Like an alchemist in the heat we cook.

Both black and saffron, mottled red and brown,
Metallic inmate, neither verb nor noun,
Does it matter to you that we shall drown?
Heavy is the body that bears the crown.
In mourning in the furnace, bolt upright,
Amid the stench of graves I reached the light;
Entwined the funnelweb; wound toward its height,
Sped the azure Savior, primrose then white.

As if I had said to the god Who goes,
Or selfsame multiverse the god Who grows,
Sum of infinity the god Who flows,
How may I realize the god Who knows?
A foetus in the googolsphere I slept,
A wanderer through hyperspace I crept,
An astronaut that large adept I stepped,
Into *the path of least action* I leapt.

THE POWER OF LIFE

Converted foam, conglomerate nations,
In the funnel virtual rotations,
The void that but the vacuum rations,
Nothing are we: quantum fluctuations.
Between the sin and compline in the din
Titanic as Our Savior's origin,
Both in and out of Creation we spin,
Decay away, then like His Cheshire grin.

Entering in space in bunting we toddle,
The infant that Yahweh yet may coddle.
What *if* Our Father scatter His dottle—
Still we mirror Him; like Gaia's model,
Unit maneuvering at the throttle
In flickers of light and shadow, mottle
Jesus' coheir, whether clay or pottle
Wry in his make as some hollow bottle.

Without a father he could not exist,
Without a mother—side lanced like a cyst,
Sublunary vessel—had never hissed,
Nor risen from her krater through its mist
Even as a cloudform: round as a wife,
Isaac at the altar; priest with his knife;
Christ at His tau-cross; goatfoot with his fife
Indestructible by the power of life.

THE QUANTUM ALICE

In the opposite direction facing,
Walking backward along yet still pacing,
Twin phantoms, in tandem interlacing,
Collided, crisscrossed, at random racing,
Scattered Alice as if she had splintered,
By that bleak and blighted skyscape pintered,
In the starry void chaotic sintered,
Taunted by a trillion atoms wintered.

Entwining the light we pass through a slit:
Crack in the fescue, eyeball that we knit,
Burrow in the midden, gap in the pit,
Chink in the cauldron, keyhole that we quit.
Outside the cavern, crescent where we sit,
She issues from Her nimbus Holy Writ:
Scroll like a boa, hand that leprous lit,
Wave's interference, insight infinite.

Gossamer particles hit on a screen
Devised by Eve's mechanic. She is keen,
Indicates possession as with a lien,
Expresses what we have or have not seen:
Some simple truth conglomerate as *pi*.
And thus might Alice spy, yet would not sigh,
Preferred the least action, happened to hie,
Fumbled, mumbled, crumbled, *ghost-kissed* the die.

THE ROUND CHAOS

To become ourselves we become concrete.
Like Hermes Trismegistus, from his seat
He mounts the universe, then scans his sheet,
Each word's velocity, like light or heat,
Such snow as flies, an iridescent ray
That burgeons in its orbit more each day,
Some Johannine image, substance that gray,
Stray infinity, he must stand away.

Recourse of atoms that space encases,
He threads the skein till it interlaces.
All-inclusive magus, still he traces.
Trefoil coheir, Process beggars Stasis.
By dint of the Cross He centers the span;
Pneumatic in Eden, enters the clan;
Shaman of nuptials, Virgin in the plan,
He takes this woman when He takes this man.

I am a migrant to another world,
Stochastic a dot in the cosmos swirled,
Martian, Venusian, in the vessel curled,
Hermetic when on *the round chaos* whirled
I race toward the moon in my crystal pod,
Galumph across the disk yet do not plod.
Unit in space, my suit an eerie sod,
Shade encased in glass I wheel before God.

SATURN'S GRAMOPHONE

When molecules surprise me in the sky,
I think beyond a cloud to flakes that fly,
Dendritic forms that dazzle me, then die.
Arrows on the target centered yet sigh.
Complexity's king, like a playground swing,
Saturn's gramophone, Iris' braided ring,
Motion in the mantle, dust on the wing,
Ge's orb-weaver's web as foamy as string.

Elsewhen in Spacetime Repetition's queen.
She sculpts an organ suited to its gene.
An eye concentric even as its sheen,
She multiplies *clear-sighted* what we mean.
Over and over She twines the same scene.
Thus She plies Her sickle, hackle, or peen,
Harvests its keen, then scatters what we glean:
This *implicate order* husked like a bean.

We train upon the sky a Cyclops' strobe,
Deploy in the heavens flyby or probe,
Eject from Her cusp the god in its lobe,
Twice bisect His sand, then curve like a globe.
Primordial hierophants we dispart,
Aim the shafts of Eros, without a chart
Raven the planets, commandeer the cart,
Dying wound none but ourselves with the dart.

SERVANT OF NATURE

Eve betrayed the Lord; then Adam, sated,
Thrust from Paradise, his sojourn slated,
Undertook the way; his token rated,
Cain revenged the gift; King David, baited,
Sacrificed the Hittite; Jonah hated—
Human consciousness *that* self-inflated
Till Our Savior curved, His hourglass mated,
Even Simon swerved, his spirit crated.

I glimpse them in their pews, not barren—round,
As swollen as a globe or as a mound:
Luna at midpoint, Hecate in the ground,
Biform Mars or Venus, polestar or hound;
At the sign of peace, by their spouses wound,
Like Eve to cosmosgonic Adam bound;
Saba her sovereign; sponsored, numbered, nouned,
Mary Her monarch, still by passion crowned.

However Gaea's banner may have twirled,
Servant of Nature, ithyphallic, burled,
Like the moon embosomed, bisected, pearled
Even as a satellite, He has hurled—
Hermetic in His capsule, buoyed or furled—
In a weightless sea till self-heated, whirled,
He colonized bliss, like a foetus curled,
Then raised us past the limits of this world.

THE SET-UP

Python of Apollo, spool in the sand
Ringed with salmon pink; His pelican fanned;
Both crane and heron mounted on a stand
Like Heaven's scarab; Goshen; Ophir's land.
Galactic hominid, Olduvai's hand;
Circle twice bisected, Galilee's strand;
Our Father's treasure, sifted contraband;
Our Savior's manna, sun and moon trepanned.

Adam and Eve assimilate the quince;
In waters composite the axe head sprints;
Across the tree of life the hammer dints.
Heart of the tincture, hyacinthine Prince,
He rests His tabernacle in its rinse.
His disks, embedded in eclipse, evince
What myrtle in the arbor regnant hints.
Lady, like Hephaestus, you make me wince.

Spun out of dust the ball on which we ride
Hurtles in Spacetime, hierophants astride
A tower of turtles down which we slide
Each lunar cycle till we scale the bride,
Enclose the loop, then self-excited bide
In mystic Oneness. Mind cannot divide.
So, this is the set-up. Nobody lied.
Blind Pharisee! Clean first the cup inside.

SPACETIME'S HANDKERCHIEF

When a gosling, Spirit-born yet tender;
Vague my soul, indifferent to gender,
I saw an artifex like a vender
Hypnotize a body, then suspend her,
With a flourish sweep his cape and send her
Out of Time and Space; as if to mend her,
Rouse her counterpart, but not to end her—
Raise the man, then woman like a mentor.

Jesus knew His target: None but the heart
Satisfied His hierophant or His dart.
Lance to the wafer, cross-piece at the start,
Compass in the chaos—these too an art.
At the Place of the Skull He climbed on splints.
He has sped us to Eden ever since.
See the glassy kingdom! There Eros sprints,
Wholeness still the door that His arrow dints.

I sensed the first path: She curved like a leaf;
Guessed the second: ghost ship or schooner's reef;
Embraced the third as the vassal His fief;
Discerned the fourth, then nudged Him like a thief;
Till I spanned the square as round as belief:
Some hood upon a tree, His mother's grief;
Cerecloth or token, Moses' scroll or sheaf;
Heaven's sudary, Spacetime's handkerchief.

SPINNER

Born of a dilemma cosmic we sprang:
Beam in the byss, then not without a pang—
Our Lord's salvific staff, despite its fang,
Afloat in space just to taste its own tang—
His spark internalized like *yin* and *yang*.
Like breath of the Bunsen, like suns that hang,
Like the eye of some cat with paws that clang,
Light rays yet seize us: candle, bulb, or bang.

Pneumatic as I whirl the hub spins by.
Vestibular pathways adjust the sky:
Plumb bob in the membrane, feet that I ply,
And still like Heracles, rotund, I try;
Collapse the icon coded in my eye;
Convey the firmament; stroll as I fly;
Petition Heaven's lap; then chthonic, shy,
Commend on high the shaman that must die.

We wander orientated to a star,
Primed as a tar or scarab in a jar;
Colubrid downward in its mystic dance,
Or, compassed, Mithras with his upcurved lance.
As Shiva and Shakti, cinctured, embrace,
In the bubble dome through Spacetime we race.
Sigil like the solstice, stone in the seal,
Griffin with its paw on the solar wheel.

SPLIT-MINDED

Made like unto God we imagine things,
Bootstrap visitations, resonant strings:
Clue in the cavern; crystals in the springs;
Precursor power vatic as a sling's;
Some heron's stone that at the threshold pings;
Chaos like a cauldron's; wheel like a king's;
Jehovah's timepiece: pendulum that swings
By His bema seat; Jerusalem's rings.

Fragile, agile, split-minded in the pan,
By contraries bound He posted the ban,
Clasped His caduceus, boarded the van,
And then like a woman compassed the man.
For, when Maria had hammered the nail,
Hypnotic the Son had knotted His tail;
Hurdled Her girdle; magic slough like kale,
Still higher spiralled, female soon and male.

Like the wise shall we enter, Word of Eve;
Even as rivers fourfold interweave,
Circulate in Spacetime; skyward yet, heave;
From Eden sprung, conceive and then believe.
The dolphin in the air exhorts its fin;
The flask on the ocean retorts its jinn;
Cloudform like a transport's, twin in the tin,
Shaman chaliced at last, he sorts the din.

TABERNACLED

I bear my body as a felon might,
Upon my back, or anywhere at night
Encapsuled by the moon, its wheel all white,
Transport my victim even as a kite
Suffused by snow, an avalanche but slight,
Primordial fire in each vas of light
Conveyed by priests or canopied in flight
Or tabernacled, in or out of sight.

A point like a seed, then particles grew
As tangible as space, the time that we rue—
Such noise inside the horn as we construe—
Not so distant that You exceed my view.
The serpent has risen, as if on cue
Shall devour His tail that round as a clue
He may portion His feast. My One, my True
Aphrodisiac, I *am* eating You.

Upraised we begin; imagine the cell;
Submersed in its membrane, float in the gel;
Eden's Monad, multiply in the well;
God's imago, hyphenate like a bell.
Conglomerate Heaven could compass Hell;
Unit wound in the void to Earth rappel;
In the vas of Her moon, His remnant swell;
Till, crowned thus in courts of Zion, we dwell.

TATTOO

He knotted the navel—this was the stunt—
Striated the belly, as was His wont;
Appeased the grasshopper, sign of the hunt;
Dispatched the riffraff; sectioned off a shunt,
The entrance to the pair—He was *that* blunt—
Impaled the fish with a pole to the bunt;
Upraised the totem; dyad with a grunt,
Urged their vital parts around to the front.

So what is a man, say, and why and who?
Son of the Son, His consort *in* the stew;
Till cut in two, then fastened with a glue,
Their androgyne—the hybrid of the dew—
Thumb like a gum, the resin of the few
Gold and red and green; tattoo "I in You"
Wheel like a heart, its flower—sapphire blue—
Etched on His flesh, quaternal, like the Jew.

In hyperspace complete, astir we greet;
Straddle the chaos; shuttlewalk His beat;
Achieve conjunction; pleasure like a bleat
Attached to the unit, melt as we meet.
A torso like a seat, it has a cleat.
A torso like a sheet, it has a pleat—
Dip at the hip; a dome, like foam, concrete:
Selene's *rebis* cinctured in the street.

TRISMEGISTUS' ART

Adrift in space, I stepped beyond the base;
Transmitted like an atom tipped the case;
Crossed the singularity; grazed my face;
In some farther harmony left my trace.
Shaman of fragments, artisan of souls,
Astral mandrake he copulates in boles;
Chalices manna; famished, harvests scrolls;
Salamander frolicking, feasts on coals.

He has heated Himself with His own heat;
Calcined His semblance; dipped His smitten feet
In liquid silver; vitrified His meat;
Restored His substance; layered sheet by sheet,
Sealed His metallic sod; His suit complete,
The *field of the square inch* His bema seat,
Grounded His *rebis*; rooted Him in peat;
His cloudform siphoned, rationed then His teat.

I glimpsed the pattern, acted, understood;
Nursed, as Adam had, His child in the yod;
Repaired to a pit like Hecate's wood;
Then twined the Sun and Moon because I could.
Molecules endure; risen atoms smart.
I lay in Her lap till I felt the dart,
Lolled exanimate, circumcised my heart,
Secured the cosmos: Trismegistus' art.

NOTES AND COMMENTS

GALACTIC PILGRIM:
NOTES AND COMMENTS
Daniel Orsini

Adam Kadmon's rite: *Adam* Kadmon is the androgynous, first-born "Son of Man" reincarnated, after the Fall, as a copy of the apocalyptic Christ. Here, his *rite*—the ground-plan of the totalistic self—refers to the "going out" of the souls from the Primordial Man—a Cabalistic doctrine—as well as to the Pauline transformation of the physical body (the first *Adam*) into the spiritual body (the second *Adam*) through the redemptive blood of Christ, the "Rubeous foetus" of line 22. See 1 Cor. 15.44-47: "If there is such a thing as an animal body, there is also a spiritual body. It is in this sense that Scripture says, 'The first man, Adam, became an animate being,' whereas the last Adam has become a life-giving spirit. [. . .] The first man was made 'of the dust of the earth': the second man is from heaven" (*The New English Bible with the Apocrypha* [1961; New York: Oxford UP, 1972]). Subsequent Biblical citations are from this ecumenical text. *Crystal*

All heaven but a readout like a map: The Divine Plan "given by God to Jesus Christ" (Rev. 1.1) is compared both to the radio transmission of pictures from a spacecraft and to the charts or tables of a collection of maps. *Liquid Metal Man*

All-inclusive magus: See Witness Lee, "The Glory of God and the Glorification of the Believers," *Affirmation and Critique* 7.1 (Apr. 2002): 11: "In God's firstborn Son [Jesus Christ] there is God and there is also man; there is death and there is also the effectiveness of death; there is resurrection and there is also the power of resurrection. He has everything in Him. This all-inclusive One now lives in us. Do we want God? He is here. [. . .] Our whole being is God." *The Round Chaos*

And then His star man: a syntactical pun, with *man* uttered as either an appositive, or an apostrophe, or an exclamation. *Citizen of the Cosmos*

Anna at the rite: at the circumcision of Jesus, a prophetess who "talked about the child to all who were looking for the liberation of Jerusalem" (Luke 2.38). *The Cheshire of Sense*

Antinomy's light: With this image, the speaker underscores the duality of *light*, which manifests the properties of both waves and particles. *The Foliate Pebble*

any down: the soft, fluffy feathers of the swan that repeat "the miracle of the [self-immolated] phoenix," i.e., the alchemical transformation "of the *nigredo* [blackness] into the *albedo* [whiteness]" and "of unconsciousness into 'illumination'" (C. G. Jung, *Mysterium Coniunctionis: An Inquiry into the Separation and Synthesis of Psychic Opposites in Alchemy*, trans. R. F. C. Hull [1963; Princeton: Princeton UP, 1989] 77). *Cinderdust*

Apostolates of colors: groups of believers who dispense Christ's "new Covenant" (2 Cor. 3.6) with religious observances symbolized by liturgical colors: red for the Passion of the Cross; purple for penance; green for hope; and white or gold for joy. *Apostolates*

Appeased the grasshopper, sign of the hunt: At the Creation, Yahweh foreordained the deliverance of His chosen people, even as he mollified His "demonic" instrument. Thus, in *The Bestiary of Christ*, trans. D. M. Dooling (1940; New York: Arkana-Penguin, 1992), Louis Charbonneau-Lassay observes that, in Exodus, "when Moses struck the Egyptians with ten plagues that liberated Israel, the eighth of these ordeals was a great cloud of grasshopper locusts that stripped the soil of Egypt of every green thing, and pursued the Egyptians into their houses" (353-54). *Tattoo*

apprehend His fen: Apparently, at this point in the poem, the speaker "attempts [in Jungian terms] to abolish the separation between the conscious mind and the unconscious, the real source of life, and to bring about a reunion [. . .] with the native soil of his inherited, instinctive make-up" (C. G. Jung, *Psychology and Alchemy*, trans. R. F. C. Hull [1953; Princeton: Princeton UP, 1993] 137). Thus, here, the symbol of his primordial past is a *fen*, either "an area of low, flat, marshy land," or a "swamp," or a "bog" ("Fen¹" [n.], def.). See *Webster's New World Dictionary*, 1988 ed.; unless otherwise indicated, subsequent definitions of key words are from this text. *God's Folly*

archetype: a universal pattern of thought expressed, in the psyche, as either an image or a symbol "of an unknown and incomprehensible content" (Jung, *Psychology and Alchemy* 17). *Borderline Noun*

Arms of plankton blooms: Here, *plankton* is "The usually microscopic animal and plant life found floating or drifting near the ocean or in bodies of fresh water [and] used as food by nearly all aquatic animals" ("Plankton" [n.], def.). See also Kevin W. Kelley, ed., *The Home Planet* (Mass.: Addison-Wesley, 1988) 66, where the NASA astronaut Edward G. Gibson views this phenomenon from the Skylab space station in Earth orbit: "We were able to see the plankton blooms resulting from the upwelling off the coast of Chile. The bloom itself extended along the coastline and had some long tenuous arms reaching out to sea. The arms or lines of plankton which were pushed around in a random direction, fairly well defined but fairly weak in color, contrasted with the dark blue ocean." *Inmate of Space*

Aroused the lame: See Luke 5.18-25: At Capernaum, after he had chastised the lawyers and the Pharisees, Jesus turned to the paralytic and said, "'I say to you, stand up, take your bed, and go home.' And at once he rose to his feet before their eyes, took up the bed he had been lying on, and went home praising God." (The miracle of the paralytic at Capernaum is also recounted in Matt. 9.2-7 and Mark 2.1-12.) *An Image of an Image*

artisan of souls: God's earthly surrogate—the alchemist—or, for that matter, any world-creating hierophant or mystagogue of light (C. G. Jung, *Alchemical Studies*, trans. R. F. C. Hull [1967; Princeton: Princeton UP, 1983] 197). See also John 10.35:

"'Those are called gods to whom the word of God was delivered—and Scripture cannot be set aside.'" *Trismegistus' Art*

As even the god entwined in its lobe: The speaker imagines that God gestates either in a fissure-like subdivision of the human brain or in the womb of Mary, the Mother of Jesus. To picture the convolutions of the brain, see Lennart Nilsson and Jan Lindberg, *Behold Man: A Photographic Journey of Discovery inside the Body*, trans. Ilona Munck (1973; Boston: Little, Brown, 1974) 162-63. *Eros' Meal*

ash: Jung explores the alchemical meaning and interpretation of *ash*, in *Mysterium Coniunctionis*: "As the alchemists strove to produce an incorruptible 'glorified body,' they would, if they were successful, attain that state in the *albedo*, where the body became spotless and no longer subject to decay. The white substance of the ash was therefore described as the 'diadem of the heart,' and its synonym, the white foliated earth (*terra alba foliata*), as the 'crown of victory.'" In addition, the *ash* was "identical with the 'pure water,'" interchangeable with *vitrum* (glass)—"which, on account of its incorruptibility and transparency, seemed to resemble [the spirit that indwells] the glorified body"—and "associated with salt [and with fire]." Thus, "the evangelist Mark had said [in 9.49] that 'every one shall be salted with fire, and every sacrifice shall be salted with salt'" (238-39). *Cinderdust*

As Hermes observes: In this stanza, the speaker functions, like the alchemical *Hermes*, as both mystagogue and *rebis*. *Courtship*

As if I had swung from atom to wave: a reference to *wave*-particle duality and the spooky reality that we inhabit—"a maelstrom of fleeting, ghostly images" (Paul Davies, *God and the New Physics* [New York: Simon, 1983] 102). *A Cloud in Slow Motion*

as if to mend her, / Rouse her counterpart: either a reversal of the order in which God created Adam and Eve or the magician's conjuration of Eve's animus "from the dark hinterland of the psyche" (C. G. Jung, *Two Essays on Analytical Psychology*, trans. R. F. C. Hull [1953; Princeton: Princeton UP, 1977] 210). According to Jung, "The animus is the deposit, as it were, of all [of] woman's ancestral experiences of man" (209), whereas the anima is "An inherited collective image of woman [that] exists in a man's unconscious" (190). *Spacetime's Handkerchief*

As I shift the blind: as I reset the horizontal slats of the venetian blind—i.e., in order to admit varying rays of light. *Elapid's Cowl*

As Shiva (*she*-vuh) and Shakti (*shuck*-tee), cinctured, embrace: In *The Archetypes and the Collective Unconscious*, trans. R. F. C. Hull (1959; Princeton: Princeton UP, 1990), C. G. Jung observes that "Shiva, according to Tantric doctrine, is the One Existent, the Timeless in its perfect state. Creation begins when this unextended point—known as *Shiva-bindu*—appears [either] in the eternal embrace of its feminine side, the Shakti" (356) or—as Jung affirms elsewhere—in an aura of "androgynous unity" tantamount to divine bliss (Jung, *Mysterium Coniunctionis* 405). *Spinner*

Astride the chaos: Cf. Jung, *Psychology and Alchemy* 244, fig. 125: The sun-moon hermaphrodite, or *rebis*, stands on the round *chaos*, the latter globe not unlike the Hermetic vas, "a kind of matrix or uterus from which the *filius philosophorum*, the miraculous stone, is to be born [...]" (237). *A Cloud in Slow Motion*

***Atropos* (*at*-roh-*pahs*)**: in Greek and Roman mythology, one of the three Fates, the sister of Clotho (*kloh*-thoh) and Lachesis (*lack*-uh-sis). *Atropos* cuts the thread of life that Clotho spins and that Lachesis measures. *Entwining the Light*

At Skull Place savors Her; where He has lain, / Apperceives Her Presence: a variation on the myth of the Gnostic Christ, the exemplar of "masculine spirituality," Who "perceives the sufferings of Sophia (i.e., the psyche) and thereby gives [H]er form and existence" (Jung, *Alchemical Studies* 335). Thus, at a hillock called Golgotha—"which means 'Place of a skull'" (Matt. 27.33)—the dying Jesus, fastened to a cross, experiences His feminine side through a projection, in Jungian terms, of His anima, an archetype represented in this octet by Mary, primal Virgin Mother as well as chosen Co-Redemptrix. *Living in Curved Space*

Attached to the unit: i.e., to the Manned Maneuvering Unit (MMU), a jetpack propulsion system that the Shuttle astronaut "latches to the hard-shell torso" of his spacesuit and operates, untethered, during satellite repair and recovery. See Joseph P. Allen and Russell Martin, *Entering Space: An Astronaut's Odyssey* (New York: Stewart, 1984) 113: "Designed in true futuristic Buck Rogers style, the MMU resembles a backpack with armrests, or some kind of overstuffed rocket chair." Deemed risky, the MMU has been replaced since 1994 by the Simplified Aid for EVA Rescue (SAFER), a small, mobility-aiding back harness worn during spacewalks and used in case of emergency only. *Tattoo*

At the Place of the Skull He climbed on splints: At Golgotha, Jesus mounted the Cross, here imaged by the speaker as two intertwined strips of wood, each of them surgical and healing. *Spacetime's Handkerchief*

the axe head sprints: the floating *axe head* that prefigures the resurrected Christ. Cf. 2 Kings 6.1-7: "A company of prophets said to Elisha, 'You can see that this place where our community is living, under you as its head, is too small for us. Let us go to the Jordan and each fetch a log, and make ourselves a place to live in.' The prophet agreed. Then one of them said, 'Please, sir, come with us.' 'I will', he said, and he went with them. When they reached the Jordan, they began cutting down trees; but it chanced that, as one man was felling a trunk, the head of his axe flew off into the water. 'Oh, master!' he exclaimed, 'it was a borrowed one.' 'Where did it fall?' asked the man of God. When he was shown the place, he cut off a piece of wood and threw it in and made the iron float. Then he said, 'There you are, lift it out.' So he stretched out his hand and took it." In *The Set-Up*, not inappropriately, the raised iron *sprints* like the model Christian of 1 Tim. 6.12: "Run the great race of faith and take hold of eternal life." *The Set-Up*

***Barnacle*:** "any member of various orders of saltwater cirriped [or curl-footed] crustaceans that cement themselves to rocks, wharves, [and] ship bottoms [. . .]" ("Barnacle" [n.], def. 2). In line 6, the Acorn *Barnacle* is so-called because, in its shell, it resembles an acorn in its cupule (*kyoo*-pyool), i.e., in the cup-shaped whorl at its base. *Heterotic*

***Beam in the byss*:** Cf. Carl Sagan, *The Cosmic Connection: An Extraterrestrial Perspective* (New York: Anchor-Doubleday, 1973) 250: In the aftermath of the Big Bang, "The gas ball had turned on," and "The first star was formed," and "There was light on the face of the heavens." Here, *byss* is an abridged form of "abyss," i.e., "the primeval void or chaos before the Creation" ("Abyss" [n.], def. 4). *Spinner*

***A bearded beehive, a hooded hollow, / The queen departs, and death-duels follow*:** an image of the ongoing renewal of life through biologically coded mating practices. In *Sexual Selection* (New York: Scientific American, 1989), James L. Gould and Carol Grant explain that "Drone honey bees [. . .] have about twice the muscle mass of queens, and roughly three times as many facets in their eyes; Darwin correctly guessed that these specializations reflect the need of competing males to spot a flying queen from as far away as possible" and to pursue her "as fast as possible" (93). See also *The Urban Naturalist* (New York: Wiley, 1987) 91, where Steven D. Garber observes that "Most honey bees [. . .] live in artificial hives, but swarms regularly escape and establish wild hives, usually in hollow trees." *Elapid's Cowl*

***Belvedere* and *Sachem* (*say*-chum):** *Belvedere* Drive and *Sachem* Drive in Cranston, Rhode Island. The specific and detailed (albeit evanescent) phenomena pictured in this octet contrast with the amorphous twilit sky described in the last stanza. *Elapid's Cowl*

***bema* (*be*-muh) *seat*:** the Judgment Seat of Christ, where the righteous shall be rewarded. In Rom. 14.10, "We shall all stand before God's tribunal"—even His redeemed believers. *The End of Ourselves; Gamonymous; Navel; Split-Minded; Trismegistus' Art*

***berm*:** a narrow ledge alongside a paved road. *Galactic Pilgrim*

***between / Space and His trace*:** During the Holy Sacrifice of the Mass, at the consecration of the two species of Bread and Wine, we "leave this world" and, mystically as well as sacramentally, "go to the Father" (John 13.1). *An Image of an Image*

***Between the sin and compline in the din*:** between the Fall of Adam and Eve and "the last of the seven canonical hours" (i.e., "night prayer") recited in the aftermath of the big bang ("Compline" [n.], def.). *The Power of Life*

***Biform astronaut*:** an epithet that alludes not only to the twofold design of the Shuttle spacesuit, with lower as well as upper torso, but also to the commingled nature—divine no less than human—of the astronaut thus enclosed. *Hourglass*

Bird of Hermes: in alchemy, not only the "solar point" and "the mercurial serpent" (Jung, *Alchemical Studies* 152), but also the immortal peacock, which "stands for all colours" because, in esoteric tradition, it "occupies the highest place as a symbol of the Holy Ghost, in whom the male-female polarity of the hermaphrodite and the Rebis is integrated" (Jung, *Mysterium Coniunctionis* 287-88). *Crystal*

Blind Pharisee! Clean first the cup inside: Cf. Matt. 23.25-26: "'Alas for you, lawyers and Pharisees, hypocrites! You clean the outside of cup and dish, which you have filled inside by robbery and self-indulgence! Blind Pharisee! Clean the inside of the cup first; then the outside will be clean also.'" In *The Set-Up*, of course, the repentant speaker addresses himself. *The Set-Up*

Bootstrap visitations: mystical states generated by the human brain. See Erich Harth, *Windows on the Mind: Reflections on the Physical Basis of Consciousness* (New York: Morrow, 1982) 117-18: "Comparisons between brains and computers are often misleading, but the loading of the bootstrap [the initial set of instructions that renders the computer operative] is probably a good analogue to the transformations that take place in the human brain. In the case of the brain, however, it is often difficult to say how much is built-in design and how much the bootstrap of early experience." *Split-Minded*

borderline noun: In *Psychology and Alchemy*, Jung reminds us that, "Owing to the fundamentally indefinable nature of human personality, the self must remain a borderline concept, expressing a reality to which no limits can be set" (355n13). *Borderline Noun*

***boson* (*boh-sahn*):** a subatomic particle; a "hypothetical packet of gravity [that] has two units of spin." The term suggests "hidden symmetries of unseen dimensions," an idea that Michio Kaku underscores in *Hyperspace: A Scientific Odyssey through Parallel Universes, Time Warps, and the Tenth Dimension* (New York: Oxford UP, 1994) 144. *Elapid's Cowl*

Both crane and heron mounted on a stand: The speaker pairs the *crane* and the *heron*, ancient symbols of longevity and wisdom respectively. See Charbonneau-Lassay, *The Bestiary of Christ* 268, 272. *The Set-Up*

Both in and out of Creation we spin, / Decay away, then like His Cheshire grin: According to the probabilistic nature of the new physics, "the observer in the quantum-mechanical world" not only "manipulates," but also "participates" in every event that he perceives. He may even inhabit separate yet parallel realities. As Harth demonstrates in *Windows on the Mind*, "The situation has been described by a bizarre example known as 'Schrödinger's cat' [after the Austrian physicist Erwin Schrödinger (1887-1961)]. This hapless creature [the equally eerie counterpart of Alice's vanishing *Cheshire* cat] is locked in a box with a 'hellish contraption' consisting of a small amount of radioactive substance, a Geiger counter, a hammer rigged to be released by the counter, and a glass vial of cyanide placed to be broken by the hammer. The sequence of events is thus: particle from decay of radioactive substance triggers Geiger counter, Geiger counter trips hammer, hammer smashes vial, cyanide escapes and kills cat."

However, "In the absence of an observation, the *complete* quantum-mechanical description of the radioactive substance would be that it has both decayed and *not* decayed, [with] the counter both tripped and not tripped, the hammer both up and down, the vial both smashed and intact, the cat both dead and alive." In short, given the Copenhagen or solipsistic view of quantum mechanics, "Only when [you] look is the matter decided one way or the other [. . .]." By contrast, given the many-universes interpretation, "The moment you open the box to check on Schrödinger's cat, there will be two different worlds, one in which you observe a healthy cat jumping out of the box, the other in which *another you* finds the cat poisoned" (223-24). *The Power of Life*

Both round as a soul's and square as a knoll's: See Jung, *Mysterium Coniunctionis* 140: "In the [Greek] magic papyri, Hermes [the god of revelation] is invoked as follows: 'O Hermes, ruler of the world, thou who dwellest in the heart, circle of the moon, round and square'" (qtd. in Karl Preisendanz, *Papyri Graecae Magicae: Die griechischen Zauberpapyri*, vol. 2 [Berlin: Teubner, 1931] 139). Jung adds that, even in the Middle Ages, the soul, like the moon, was "believed to be round." Here, of course, the *square* knoll is the hill of Golgotha, not only the site of Christ's crucifixion, but also a symbol of "the four quarters of the world" (Jung, *Psychology and Alchemy* 132). *In the Line of Melchizedek*

both small and vast: Cf. Jung's statement on the "metamorphosis of the gods" in *The Archetypes and the Collective Unconscious* 157-58: As an archetypal God-image, "the still-living 'Christ-child' [. . .] has the typical feature of being 'smaller than small and bigger than big.'" *Citizen of the Cosmos*

Bow in the cloud: Cf. Gen. 9.8-14: "God spoke to Noah and to his sons with him: [. . .] 'My bow [i.e., my rainbow] I set in the cloud, / sign of the covenant / between myself and earth. / When I cloud the sky over the earth, / the bow shall be seen in the cloud.'" *Heir Presumptive*

Brahma (brah-muh): in the Hindu religion, "the supreme and eternal essence or spirit of the universe" ("Brahma" [n.], def. 1). *Orpheus' Rite*

Bread in the chalice for the first time fresh: Having internalized—i.e., having meditated upon—the mystery of transubstantiation, the speaker appreciates, with new awareness, "[t]he infinite value of the Body and Blood of Christ and the infinite power of His charity," for, in Christ, humankind "becomes once again supernaturally pleasing to God and capable of union with Him" (Thomas Merton, *The Living Bread* [1956; New York: Dell, 1959] 62). *Inmate of Space*

bryozoans (bry-uh-zoh-unz): tiny aquatic animals that attach their mosslike colonies to stones and seaweed and reproduce by budding. *Bio*

Bulbous as an hourglass: The speaker underscores both the feminine roundness and the spatiotemporal mortality of his surrogate Hermes. *Eros' Meal*

***Bulky cumuli boil across the bay*:** a climactic image of Nature's blind persistence. As Richard Scorer and Arjen Verkaik demonstrate in *Spacious Skies* (London: David & Charles, 1989), "In most cases cumulus [clouds] form during the day, evaporate by evening and are absent during the night" (39). *Elapid's Cowl*

***the Bunsen*:** a shortened form of the compound noun *Bunsen burner*, "a small gas burner that produces a hot, blue flame, [a device] used in chemistry laboratories [. . .]" ("Bunsen burner," def.). *Spinner*

***bunt*:** the mid-section of a fishing net that, pouchlike, holds the catch. *Tattoo*

***bunting*:** a "baby's garment of soft, warm cloth made into a kind of hooded blanket that can be closed, exposing only the face" ("Bunting[1]" [n.], def. 3). *The Power of Life*

***burble da or ma*:** to gurgle or babble the infantile words for father and mother, as a child does. *Orpheus' Rite*

***burn, then spurn their metals*:** [Cabiri] heat [the remnants of the day], then reject the earthly substance. Here, like alchemists, Nature's chthonic gods seek to transmute base (twilit) *metals* into gold. *Elapid's Cowl*

***Burrow in the midden*:** the tunnel-like rabbit hole from *Alice's Adventures in Wonderland*, but here dug either in a mound or in a prehistoric "refuse heap" ("Midden" [n.], def. 1). *The Quantum Alice*

***But what was I doing out of my grave?*:** The speaker himself is momentarily "overpowered by the archaic forces of the unconscious" (Jung, *Psychology and Alchemy* 329). *A Cloud in Slow Motion*

By beasts, and birds, and things that creep: Cf. Hos. 2.18: "Then I will make a covenant on behalf of Israel with the wild beasts, the birds of the air, and the things that creep on the earth, and I will break bow and sword and weapon of war and sweep them off the earth, so that all living creatures may lie down without fear." *Courtship*

By Jesus salted: Cf. not only Jung, *Mysterium Coniunctionis* 246, where the German alchemist Johann Rudolf Glauber (1604-1670) "says that his favorite disciple John was 'salted with the salt of wisdom,'" but also Mark 9.49 (AV), where the Messiah promises that "'every one shall be salted with fire, and every sacrifice shall be salted with salt'" (239). For Glauber, "Christ is the salt of wisdom which is given at baptism" (241). *Crystal*

by the way of His flesh: In Heb. 10.19-20, the coheirs of the all-inclusive Christ may seek—and obtain—a personal encounter with the Father because "the blood of Jesus makes us free to enter boldly into the sanctuary [i.e., the tent of His priesthood] by the new, living way which he has opened for us through the curtain, the way of his flesh." See also Merton, *The Living Bread* 62: "It is clear that in the sacrifice of the Mass we come into the closest possible contact with the Body of Christ, the author of all sanctification, in the very act by which He takes away the sins of the world. This is truly an objective Atonement." *Inmate of Space*

Cabiri (kuh-*beer*-ee): misshapen dwarf gods. (The singular form of the noun is Cabir.) According to Jung, as "kinsmen of the unconscious," the *Cabiri* "protect navigation, [. . .] the venture into darkness and uncertainty." Jung adds that, although "they stand in grotesque contrast to the heavenly gods," the *Cabiri* "are actually to be found on Olympus; for they are eternally striving from the depths to the heights and are therefore always to be found both below and above" (*Psychology and Alchemy* 157-58). *Elapid's Cowl; The End of Ourselves*

caduceus (ka-*doo*-see-us): in Greek mythology, the wingèd staff, with two serpents twined around it, that Hermes (the messenger of the gods) carried. *Split-Minded*

Calcined His bones: The speaker conjures up a process of alchemical transformation called "the quartering of the philosophy": the *nigredo* (the blackening), the *albedo* (the whitening), the *citrinitas* (the yellowing), and the *rubedo* (the reddening). Significantly, "since the beginning of the Christian era," the "desired goal" of the alchemists had been neither more nor less than the "chymical wedding" of the red King and the white Queen, the crowned hermaphrodite. However, in *God's Folly*, evidently, at this stage of the regeneration mystery, "The calcination [. . .] corresponds to incineration." (See Jung, *Psychology and Alchemy* 228-32, 402n172.) *God's Folly*

Calcined His semblance: The pronoun referent—whether Prajapati, Christ, or the ascetic speaker—could "burn to ashes or powder" the sole object of his transformation: himself ("Calcine" [vt.], def. 2). As Jung shows in *Alchemical Studies*, the immortal body must be "melted out" (21). *Trismegistus' Art*

Canopus' (kuh-*know*-pus) copy: a supergiant binary star. In the southern December sky, *Canopus* may appear fainter than Sirius but is actually brighter and has a higher temperature. *Eros' Meal*

Capricorn: a constellation—called the "Sea Goat"—shaped like a large, faint triangle and regarded by the ancients as the Gate of Heaven (Sune Engelbrektson, *Stars, Planets, and Galaxies* [New York: Ridge-Bantam, 1975] 36). *Heir Presumptive*

Castor's van: here, a celestial spaceship. In many accounts of the Greek and Roman myth, Castor, the mortal twin of the immortal Pollux, represents the hyphenated God-man, since he lives half of each year on earth and half in heaven. *Living in Curved Space*

Celestial utterance, point that I span: According to the Gnostics, the Original (hermaphroditic) Man is not only the undivided point "present in the body," but also "the utterance of God" in human form (C. G. Jung, *Aion: Researches into the Phenomenology of the Self*, trans. R. F. C. Hull [1959; Princeton: Princeton UP, 1969] 198-99). In the Brihadaranyaka Upanishad 1.4.3, *purusha*—the parallel in India of the cosmic Anthropos of Gnosticism—is "'as large as a man and woman embracing'" (qtd. in Jung, *Psychology and Alchemy* 161). *Living in Curved Space*

Centaurus A: Discovered in 1826 by the Scottish astronomer James Dunlop, *Centaurus A* is "a giant elliptical galaxy [in the southern constellation of *Centaurus*, the Centaur] currently in the process of devouring a [smaller] dusty barred spiral galaxy." (See *Constellation Guide: Centaurus A* 12 Oct. 2014: 4 <www.constellation-guide.com/centaurus-a>.) *Courtship*

cephalopod** (**sef**-uh-luh-**pod**) **mollusks: such marine animals as the octopus, squid, and cuttlefish. Most species carry an ink sac that contains a dark fluid activated for protection or defense. *Bio*

Cepheid: "any of a class of pulsating, yellow, supergiant stars whose brightness varies in regular periods: from the period-luminosity relation, the distance of such a star can be determined" ("Cepheid [variable]" [n.], def.). *Courtship*

cerecloth: Jesus' shroud as well as "the ghostly imprint faintly visible on the cloth itself" (Ian Wilson, *Jesus: The Evidence* [Washington, DC: Regnery, 2000] 134). *Liquid Metal Man*

Cerecloth or token: Christ's shroud—the "clean linen sheet" of Matt. 27.59—construed here as either "a sign, indication, or symbol" of the Savior's affection or as a lover's "keepsake" ("Token" [n.], defs. 1, 4a). *Spacetime's Handkerchief*

chafers: various beetles—including the cockchafer and the rose chafer—that ravage plants. *Bio*

Chalices manna: The believer-priest, being tabernacled, contains within himself the spiritual food of God. *Trismegistus' Art*

chasuble: the outer priestly vestment that, originally, "was a very full garment, shaped like a bell and reaching almost to the feet all the way round" (*Saint Joseph Daily Missal* [New York: Catholic Book, 1959] 10). *Apostolates*

Cheshire: the eerie cat that vanishes with a grin in Lewis Carroll's *Alice's Adventures in Wonderland*. *The Cheshire of Sense; Cinderdust; Elapid's Cowl; Galactic Pilgrim; Heir Presumptive; Inmate of Space; Jack-o'-Lantern; Liquid Metal Man; The Power of Life*

Cheshire like the planet blue, white, and gray: The speaker realizes that, one day, like the grinning cat from Lewis Carroll's *Alice's Adventures in Wonderland*, Earth itself will disappear. Of course, in this context, the *Cheshire* may also refer to "Schrödinger's cat," the weird creature that, according to "the [Everett-DeWitt] many-worlds interpretation" of quantum mechanics, exists in "two or more different realities" at the same time (Harth, *Windows on the Mind* 223-25). *Inmate of Space*

Christ astride the chaos with His ballasts: Cf. Jung, *Psychology and Alchemy*

324, fig. 164: "Mercurius, standing on the round chaos, holding the scales which signify the *pondus et mensura.*" See also Lev. 19.36-37: "You shall have true scales, true weights, true measures dry and liquid. I am the Lord your God who brought you out of Egypt. You shall observe all my rules and laws and carry them out." *Bio*

Cimmerian: dim or gloomy, like the dwelling place of the Cimmerians, "a mythical people whose land was described by Homer as a region of perpetual mist and darkness" ("Cimmerian" [adj.], def.). *The Crowned Hermaphrodite*

Cinctured Asclepius: "the Greek god of healing, who, while still a mortal, raised a man from the dead and was struck by a thunderbolt as a punishment" (C. G. Jung, *Symbols of Transformation*, trans. R. F. C. Hull [1956; Princeton: Princeton UP, 1990] 239). The speaker, like *Asclepius* a sharer in the divine life, wears the priestly cincture, a cord or belt of cloth that encircles his waist and that represents the virtues of chastity and continence. Here, the cincture also recalls the visible seam or suture with which the opposites (e.g., light/darkness; consciousness/unconsciousness) are united, as in the symbol of the hermaphrodite. By contrast, in the higher Adam, "the opposition is invisible" (Jung, *Aion* 248). *The Foliate Pebble*

cinctured in the street: Girded with a cord or belt of cloth that signifies the virtues of chastity and self-restraint, the Space Shuttle astronaut may yet reach his destination: a *street* of "pure gold, like translucent glass," in the holy city of Jerusalem (Rev. 21.21). *Tattoo*

A cinctured suit: the clamped torso of an astronaut's spacesuit compared to the belted alb of a priest's Mass vestments. In the Roman Catholic Church, the cord or cincture worn around the waist symbolizes the virtues of chastity and self-control. *Bowknot*

cinderdust: a fragment or remnant of ash, the product of an essential stage in alchemical transformation—the calcination that "corresponds to incineration." The resulting "incandescent ash [itself] tends towards vitrification" (Jung, *Psychology and Alchemy* 401-402). The term also recaps the origin of humankind from "the nuclear processes in the insides of the stars," a "fable" that Sagan narrates in *The Cosmic Connection*: "And then one day there came to be a creature whose genetic material was in no way different from the self-replicating molecular collectives of any other organisms on his planet, which he called Earth. But he was able to ponder the mystery of his origins, the strange and tortuous path by which he had emerged from star-stuff. He was the matter of the cosmos, contemplating itself [. . .]. He was one of the starfolk. And he longed to return to the stars" (255). *Cinderdust*

Circle twice bisected: the Christian sojourner framed as a circumscribed human cross. Cf. Jung, *The Archetypes and the Collective Unconscious* 382: "it is evident that individuation, or becoming whole, is neither a *summum bonum* nor a *summum desideratum*, but the painful experience of the union of opposites. That is the real meaning of the cross in the circle [. . .]." *The Set-Up*

***circumcised my heart*:** Being Christ-centered, the speaker has striven to "cleanse [himself] from sin" so that he may "purify" his eros ("Circumcise" [vt.], def. 2). Cf. Andrew Murray, *The Spirit of Christ* (Pennsylvania: Whitaker House, n.d.) 186: "The believer must realize that there is nothing in which the power of the flesh can assert itself more than in the activity of the mind in its dealing with the divine Word. [...] He needs to ask for the circumcised ear: the ear in which the fleshly power of the understanding has been removed. Then the Spirit of the life in Christ Jesus [that pulsates] within the heart [of the petitioner] can listen with the [selfsame indwelt] obedience of the life, even as Christ did [listen]." *Trismegistus' Art*

Citizen of the cosmos born at last: Jesus endlessly defined and redefined through "the growth of the human personality" and through "the development of consciousness" (Jung, *Aion* 221). To punctuate this idea, Jung cites "a theological opinion: [...] 'Jesus is still in the making'" (221n157). [The original source is R. Roberts, "Jesus or Christ?—A Reply," *The Quest*, vol. 2 (London, 1911) 124.] *Citizen of the Cosmos*

***A city like a crystal, End-time's town*:** Cf. Rev. 21.10-11: At the end of the world, "the holy city of Jerusalem" shall come "down out of heaven from God" with "the radiance of some priceless jewel, like a jasper, clear as crystal." *Borderline Noun*

***Clapper in the fracas*:** a paraphrase of Rev. 9.13-17. Here, the trumpet of the sixth angel becomes the tongue of the bell that announces End-time amid "fire, smoke, and sulphur," and "squadrons of cavalry." *Astronaut*

clear-sighted: capable of "the true grasping of light" through "new capacities of mind suited to seeing" and "aligned to nature" (Arthur Zajonc, *Catching the Light: The Entwined History of Light and Mind* [1993; New York: Oxford UP, 1995] 339-40). Zajonc suggests that Paul Cézanne uses the word definitively in a letter written to his son on 8 September 1906: "'Finally, I must tell you that as a painter I am becoming more clearsighted before nature'" (338). *Saturn's Gramophone*

***cleft that we priced*:** the Virgin Mary, the "glorified" vessel of line 12. In addition, the speaker alludes not only to Mary, "the mother of my Lord," in Luke 1.43, but also to the Parable of the Pearl of Great Price, i.e., of the Holy Mother Church, in Matt. 13.45-46. Jung's assessment of the Mother Archetype in *Symbols of Transformation* is equally pertinent: "Where the roads *cross* and enter into one another, thereby symbolizing the union of opposites, there is the 'mother,' the object and epitome of all union. Where the roads *divide*, where there is parting, separation, splitting, there we find the 'division,' the cleft—the symbol of the mother and at the same time the essence of what the mother means for us, namely cleavage and farewell" (371). *Gamonymous*

Clotho (*kloh*-thoh): In Greek and Roman mythology, *Clotho*, one of the three Fates, spins the thread of life that Lachesis (*lack*-uh-sis) measures and that Atropos (*at*-roh-*pahs*) cuts. *The Crowned Hermaphrodite; A Cup of Water*

Cloverleaf: a quasar—or a *quas*(i-stell)*ar* radio source—discovered in 1988. Quasars "are thought to be the ancient, exploding origins of new galaxies and are possibly the most distant and oldest observable objects in the universe" ("Quasar" [n.], def.]. *Courtship*

Clue in the cavern: in the Greek myth, the "ball of thread" that Ariadne, the daughter of King Minos, gave to Theseus. With it, he entered the famous Labyrinth in Crete; found the Minotaur, a bull with the head and torso of a man; and then, having slain the monster that fed on human flesh, retraced his steps out of the maze. See Edith Hamilton, *Mythology* (1940; New York: Mentor-New American, 1942) 150-52. *Split-Minded*

coalfish in the swell: a dark-colored pollock fish that swims either on a large, crestless wave or in a succession of waves. *Astronaut*

Coal Sack: either of two overlapping dust clouds in the Milky Way, especially "one located near Crux [the Southern Cross, a small constellation near the celestial pole]" ("Coal Sack" [n.], def.). *Courtship*

coated as I squint: layered either in foamy sweat (Luke 22.44), in broidered linen (Exod. 28.39), or in gleaming armor (Eph. 6.10-18). Jung examines the link between the Redeemer's sweat-bath, self-incubation, and the arcane substance in *Psychology and Alchemy* 339 and also in *Alchemical Studies* 290, 295. *Liquid Metal Man*

coelacanths (*see*-la-*kanths*): a mostly extinct order of bony fishes that now claims but a single living species, the latimeria. *Bio*

Coheir of the Kingdom: Cf. Eph. 3.6: "through the Gospel the Gentiles are joint heirs with the Jews, part of the same body, sharers together in the promise [of Salvation] made in Christ Jesus." *The Foliate Pebble*

Coheir, rebis, bride of His royal ban: As a mirror of the archetypal God-image, the speaker becomes at once an heir of Christ's Kingdom, a crowned hermaphrodite, and a "prototype of the royal marriage"—i.e., a *bride* of contrasting pairs (Jung, *Psychology and Alchemy* 413). Significantly, in *Aion*, Jung defines the *rebis* as "The dual being born of the alchemical union of opposites" (masculine/feminine) and recognized "as a symbol of the self" (268). Here *ban* means both "a proclamation [of an intended marriage]" and, in regard to the bizarre concept of the *rebis*, "a prohibition" ("Ban" [n.], defs. 1, 4). *Living in Curved Space*

Coheir smitten; hierophant like a cup; / Commingled spouse and housel: the crucified and love-struck Christ imaged by the speaker as—successively—priest, Chalice, Bridegroom, and Eucharist. However, in these lines (23-24), it may be that Christ and the liquid metal man—i.e., the mercurial speaker as a member of His sealed Church—become, at the Communion rite, One and the same. See Merton, *The Living Bread* 118: "Jesus gives us His Body not merely as the principle of our own life and sanctification, but as the principle of unity in His Mystical Body. He unites us not only to Himself, [and] not only to the Father in Himself, but also to one another. This is the full 'Mystery' of the Eucharist [. . .]." *Liquid Metal Man*

coheirs that climb / Between His trees: a lunisolar image, the symbol of alchemy's "royal marriage" (or "chymical wedding") as well as of divine unity. Cf. Jung, *Psychology and Alchemy* 231, fig. 116: the "Crowned hermaphrodite representing the union of king and queen, [and standing] between the sun and moon trees." *Gamonymous*

coiled in its eye: i.e., twined around itself like Ouroboros, the snake that bites its own tail, an alchemical symbol of wholeness. *Courtship*

coil that He binds: the spiraling superstring of the cosmos—along with its vibrating "resonances"—that, in the speaker's view, only Christ can "fasten" or "secure" ("Bind" [vt.], defs. 3, 7). See Kaku, *Hyperspace* 154. *Living in Curved Space*

coitus' gum: a famous alchemical recipe ascribed to Maria Prophetissa, the legendary alchemist and reputed "sister of Moses"—"join in true marriage gum with gum." Jung indicates that "The coitus of Sol and Luna in the bath," the conjunction of male and female, "is a central mythologem in alchemy" (*Psychology and Alchemy* 401nn169-70). *The Foliate Pebble*

Collapse the icon coded in my eye: In *Catching the Light*, Zajonc discovers that, by observing the sky, the "clearsighted" perceiver reifies it as both a quantum phenomenon and an archetypal instance (296). *Spinner*

Collapse the puzzle: Like Zajonc, the speaker assumes that, by entwining the light of the mind with the light of nature, the seer brings the world—"which until then had eluded the eye"—into "clearsighted" reality (*Catching the Light* 338-39). However, what the human perceiver actualizes, in the view of the physicist John Archibald Wheeler, is a "closed-loop participatory universe," since "this same physical world generates the observers that are responsible for concretizing its existence." (Paul Davies elaborates on the latter idea in *The Mind of God: The Scientific Basis for a Rational World* [New York: Simon, 1992] 223-26.) *God's Folly*

colonized: The speaker refers to "the collective nature of the self" (Jung, *Alchemical Studies* 240)—in sum, "the One and the root of itself," an "indescribable totality" (139). *Heterotic*

Colubrid downward in its mystic dance: *downward*, because "the snake is the commonest symbol for the dark, chthonic [i.e., subterranean and/or material] world of instinct" (Jung, *Aion* 244). Serpents from the family *Colubridae* include both venomous and non-venomous types. *Spinner*

commandeer the cart: a variation on the cautionary Greek myth of Phaëthon (*fay*-uh-*thon*), the reckless offspring of the sun-god Helios (*hee*-lee-*ahs*). When Phaëthon "tries to drive his father's sun-chariot," he "almost sets the world on fire, but Zeus strikes him down with a thunderbolt" ("Phaëthon" [n.], def.). Here, of course, "primordial hierophants" arrogantly seize NASA's rocket-borne spacecraft. *Saturn's Gramophone*

***Commingled spouse and housel*, right side up:** the Christian communicant wedded to Christ in the Holy Sacrifice of the Mass, both Eucharistic chalice and nourished coheir set in an upright—i.e., a vertical or perpendicular—position. See also *Catching the Light* 31-32, where Zajonc asks a question concerning human vision—"How can the image on the retina be upside down when we see the world right side up?"—and then proceeds to answer it: "At this point optics ends and the light of the body, that is the soul's activities, must be engaged in order for us to see the world right side up." *Liquid Metal Man*

***Compass in the chaos*:** here, an instrument "for showing direction," with the sutured Cross as pivot and Christ as magnetic needle ("Compass" [n.], def. 5). See Jung, *Symbols of Transformation* 264-66, including fig. 36. *Spacetime's Handkerchief*

***Complete, illumined, purged*:** The speaker asserts that, through the indwelling Presence of the Spirit of Christ, each of His coheirs may become whole, enlightened, and redeemed. See Murray, *The Spirit of Christ* 208: "Deeper down than where the soul with its consciousness can enter, there is a spirit-nature linking man with God." *Eros' Meal*

***Complexity's king, like a playground swing*:** In *Exploring Complexity: An Introduction* (New York: W. H. Freeman, 1989), Grégoire Nicolis and Ilya Prigogine reaffirm "a new vision of matter, one no longer passive, as described in the mechanical world view, but associated with spontaneous activity" (3). Thus, "A periodically forced pendulum—such as a playground swing— [. . .] gives rise to a rich variety of motions," even random excursions into turbulence. "In short, the idea of complexity is no longer limited to biology. It is invading the physical sciences and appears to be deeply rooted in the laws of nature" (8). *Saturn's Gramophone*

***Conceived as in a capsule cannot flee*:** The speaker compares spiritual rebirth both to the Savior's physical conception in the womb and to the astronaut's spiritual transformation in a spacecraft. *Inmate of Space*

***Conglomerate God, His Sonship threefold*:** Jung clarifies this idea—the "discrimination [or separation] of the natures"—in *Aion*. According to the Gnostic teachings of Basilides [fl. AD 120-45], "The first 'son,' whose nature was the finest and most subtle, remained up above with the Father"; the second son "descended a bit lower," while the third son, "as his nature needed purifying [. . .], fell deeper into 'formlessness.'" Jung concludes that, in these three distinct epiphanies of *God*, "it is not hard to see the trichotomy of spirit, soul, and body [. . .]" (64). *Cinderdust*

Conglomerate soul: the coming Messiah, the second Adam, regarded by the Cabalists as the collective aggregate of all individual souls—as "a 'conglomerate soul,' to use the Indian expression"—and therefore, in modern analytical psychology, as a symbol of the self (Jung, *The Archetypes and the Collective Unconscious* 357). See also Jung, *Aion* 62n75: In the pre-psychological age, "Christ did not merely *symbolize* wholeness, but, as a psychic phenomenon, he *was* wholeness. [. . .] The idea of totality is, at any given time, [only] as total as one is oneself." *Crystal*

Conjugated verb-stem: the tabernacled speaker extolled as both an offspring of God and a repetition of "the Word [that] became flesh" (John 1.14). Cf. Jung, *Aion* 221n157: "'Jesus is still in the making.'" *Borderline Noun*

Conjunction at my lot: The speaker recalls his connection to Earth—and hence to humankind and the cosmos—by tracking his measured parcel of land. *Elapid's Cowl*

Conquered Gehenna (gi-hen-uh): an allusion to Christ's descent into Hell. Cf. Rom. 14.9: "This is why Christ died and came to life again, to establish his lordship over [both the] dead and [the] living." *Heterotic*

Consoled the waters: See Mark 4.37-39: "A heavy squall came on and the waves broke over the boat until it was all but swamped. Now he [Jesus] was in the stern asleep on a cushion; they roused him and said, 'Master, we are sinking! Do you not care?' He awoke, rebuked the wind, and said to the sea, 'Hush! Be still!' The wind dropped and there was a dead calm." (Jesus also calms the storm in Matt. 8.23-27 and Luke 8.22-25.) *An Image of an Image*

Converted foam, conglomerate nations: In *Other Worlds: A Portrait of Nature in Rebellion / Space, Superspace and the Quantum Universe* (New York: Simon and Schuster, 1980), Paul Davies suggests that "our world canvas" has not only texture, but also "a foam or sponge-like structure [. . .]" (96). Furthermore, "Contained in superspace are all the possible spaces—doughnuts, spheres, spaces with wormholes and bridges—each with a different froth arrangement [. . .]" (104). *The Power of Life*

copulative Ah: an ejaculatory sigh that evokes both the frenzy of sexual love and the agony of death. *Orpheus' Rite*

Corals: marine polyps that secrete rocklike deposits in tropical seas. *Bio*

Corascene (kor-uh-seen): in alchemy, "the dark, dangerous, rabid dog"—associated with the moon goddess Selene—that "changes into an eagle at the time of the plenilunium. His darkness disappears and he becomes a solar animal." In effect, the *Corascene* dog functions as a symbol both of "the reborn and sublimated Sol and Luna" and of the transformation of consciousness. See Jung, *Mysterium Coniunctionis* 154-55. *Navel*

cosmogony's hum: the static due to "the radiation left over from the fireball that filled the Universe at the beginning of its existence" (Robert Jastrow, *God and the Astronomers* [New York: Norton, 1978] 20-21). *The Foliate Pebble*

Crack in the fescue: a narrow opening in either "lawn [or] pasture grasses" ("Fescue" [n.], def. 2). *The Quantum Alice*

crescent where we sit: In *Mysterium Coniunctionis*, Jung notes that the moon is the "receptacle of souls." Thus, in Plutarch, "Hermes [the guide of souls] sits in the moon and goes round with it (just as Heracles does in the sun)" (140). *The Quantum Alice*

***Crinoids* (cry-noyds):** marine animals, some of which are shaped like flowers—e.g., the sea lily and the feather star. *Bio*

***Crossed the singularity*:** In *Space-Time and Beyond: Toward an Explanation of the Unexplainable* (New York: Dutton, 1975), Bob Toben, "in conversation" with Jack Sarfatti and Fred Wolf, explains that "Singularities are entry and exit points of *that which is beyond space-time* projecting itself into space-time" (145). Thus, in this poem, the speaker figures that he jumped "through the ring singularity in the interior of a rotating blackhole" (32) and departed Spacetime altogether. *Trismegistus' Art*

***cross-piece at the start*:** The speaker knows that, when the Christian runner undertakes his race, the Cross is a requisite prop. So Paul counsels us: "we must throw off every encumbrance, every sin to which we cling, and run with resolution the race for which we are entered, our eyes fixed on Jesus from start to finish: Jesus who, for the sake of the joy that lay ahead of him, endured the cross, making light of its disgrace [. . .]" (Heb. 12.1-2). *Spacetime's Handkerchief*

The crowned hermaphrodite: The crown is a universal symbol "equivalent to the rays of the sun"; thus, the alchemical *hermaphrodite* "is generally represented as crowned" (Jung, *Symbols of Transformation* 183-84 and pl. XVIII). See also Wisd. Sol. 5.16: "the just live for ever; their reward is in the Lord's keeping, and the Most High has them in his care. Therefore royal splendour shall be theirs, and a fair diadem from the Lord himself [. . .]." (Jung features a vivid illustration—the "Crowned hermaphrodite representing the union of king and queen" and "standing between the sun and moon trees"—in *Psychology and Alchemy* 231, fig. 116.) *A Cloud in Slow Motion; The Crowned Hermaphrodite*

***Crowned Ouroboros*:** the snake that bites its own tail—a self-described circle—as a symbol of totality. In other words, the speaker desires "a synthesis of conscious and unconscious data" (Jung, *Aion* 190). Here, appropriately enough, the mercurial serpent wears the sun-disc of a crown. *Living in Curved Space*

***crown that we braid*:** a twist on the flowery deaths and resurrections of such mythical Greek heroes as Narcissus, Hyacinthus, and Adonis. Undertaking the Way of the Cross, Christians weave for themselves the same *crown* of thorns that Yahweh prepared for Christ. *Elapid's Cowl*

***crystal pod*:** the futuristic habitat of the deployed astronaut—here, but a glassy enclosure shaped not unlike a floating "seed vessel" ("Pod" [n.], def. 1). *The Round Chaos*

***crystals in the springs*:** Christ's incorruptible believer-priests baptized in water that flows from pools or ponds. In the literature of the Church Fathers, Christ is often compared to a crystal. Thus, in his *Homiliae in Ezechielem* (*Homilies on Ezekiel*), Saint Gregory the Great [c. 540-604] explains that, through the "glory" of His resurrection, Christ "'hardened after the fashion of a crystal from water, so that there was one and the same nature in it and in [H]im [. . .]'" (qtd. in Jung, *Mysterium Coniunctionis*

449n345). *Split-Minded*

Curlicue acacia: a tree of the mimosa family with clusters of curvy yellow or white flowers. *Eros' Meal*

cyborg: "A bionic human," a hypothetical being "having normal biological capability or performance enhanced by or as if by electronic or electromechanical devices" (Peter Menzel and Faith D'Aluisio, *Robo sapiens: Evolution of a New Species* [Cambridge: MIT P, 2000] 234). *The Crowned Hermaphrodite*

a Cyclops' (sigh-klahps) strobe: the primary mirror of the Earth-orbiting Hubble Space Telescope compared to the sight of "any of a race of giants who have only one eye, in the middle of the forehead" ("Cyclops" [n.], def.). *Saturn's Gramophone*

demesne (duh-mean): the world as God's domain—here, "the land or estate belonging to a lord and not rented or let but kept in his hands" ("Demesne" [n.], def. 2). *In the Line of Melchizedek*

Dendritic forms: stellar dendrites—platelike snow crystals with both branches and sidebranches. *Saturn's Gramophone*

Describes the center: the linked or "sutured" Ouroboros projected as a symbol of the Self. The *center* is at once the celestial city of End-time, the bema-seat Jesus, and the speaker himself, Christ's implicated coheir. *Living in Curved Space*

Devonian: a geological period (408-360 million years ago) marked by an abundance of fishes and the appearance of the first amphibians and insects. The proper adjective, which derives from "Devon," a county of southwest England, is pronounced with a long "o." *Bio*

did housel what I mean: Through His intermediary—the priest officiating at Mass—Jesus housels (i.e., administers the Eucharist to) the speaker, an indwelt coheir of His kingdom. According to John 6.54, the Son of God, when teaching at a synagogue in Capernaum, made the following promise: "'Whoever eats my flesh and drinks my blood possesses eternal life, and I will raise him up on the last day.'" To savor the sense of *what I mean*, see also *Aion* 164, where Jung clarifies the significance, in alchemy, of the Latin pronouns 'quis' (who) and 'quid' (*what*): "whereas 'quis' has an unmistakably personal aspect and refers to the ego, 'quid' is neuter, predicating nothing except an object which is not endowed even with personality. Not the subjective ego-consciousness is meant, but the psyche itself as the unknown, unprejudiced object that still has to be investigated. The difference between knowledge of the ego and knowledge of the self could hardly be formulated more trenchantly than in this distinction between 'quis' and 'quid.'" *An Image of an Image*

Didymus (did-uh-muss): the apostle Thomas—called *Didymus*, "the Twin"—who refused to believe that Jesus had risen from the dead until he saw the wound. See

John 20.24-29. *In the Line of Melchizedek*

dispart: an archaic word—"to divide into parts; separate" ("Dispart" [vt., vi.], def.). *Jack-o'-Lantern; Saturn's Gramophone*

Distilled His Host: a reference to Christ's circular distillation in the Eucharistic cup. According to the speaker, this vessel rather than the alchemist's retort is "the true philosophical Pelican." See Jung, *Psychology and Alchemy* 128. *God's Folly*

divines: Spiritual conversion enables the speaker "to engage in divination," i.e., to interpret the unknown through supernatural insight ("Divine" [vi.], def. 1). *Living in Curved Space*

Dog Star: also called Sirius and Sothis (*soh*-this); the brightest star seen from Earth. In the ancient Egyptian story of Isis and Osiris—a "lunar mystery"—the rising of the *Dog Star* (i.e., of Isis manifest as the star Sothis) "brought Osiris back to life." See Anne Baring and Jules Cashford, *The Myth of the Goddess: Evolution of an Image* (New York: Viking, 1991) 233-34. *Inmate of Space*

a dome, like foam, concrete: The speaker refers not only to the actual helmet of the NASA astronaut—a clear plastic bubble covered by the Extravehicular Visor Assembly—but also to its virtual source-point: quantum *foam*. See Malcolm W. Browne, "Physicists Confirm Power of Nothing, Measuring Force of Universal Flux," where Dr. John N. Bahcall of the Institute for Advanced Study at Princeton, N.J., asserts that "We are all quantum fluctuations. [...] That's the origin of all of us and of everything in the universe, not just dark matter" (*The New York Times* 21 Jan. 1997: C6, 22 Nov. 2014: 3 <http://www.nytimes.com/1997/01/21/science/physicists-confirm-power-of-nothing-measuring-force-of-universal-flux.html?pagewanted=print>). *Tattoo*

Do my stint: [I] undertake the Way of the Cross. *Liquid Metal Man*

dot: In alchemy, the iota or indivisible point, an emblem of the holistic self, "is simple, indestructible, and eternal" (Jung, *Alchemical Studies* 186). See also Jung, *Mysterium Coniunctionis* 44n24: "The iota, the smallest Greek character," corresponds "to our 'dot' (which did not exist in Greek)." *The Round Chaos*

dottle: the lump of tobacco ash left in the bowl of a pipe after it has been smoked. Here, in His reductive anthropomorphic form, the Creator disperses the ashes from His pipe like a proud parent. *The Power of Life*

down which we slide / Each lunar cycle till we scale the bride: The image suggests both lunar eclipse and sexual consummation. *The Set-Up*

drogue: in the Apollo 11 expedition, a portion of the docking device removed—along with the hatch and the probe—to clear the tunnel between the command module and the lunar module. *Bowknot*

dyad: two entities that form a pair; a reference to the antithetical nature of the Creator—e.g., male/female; physical/spiritual (Jung, *Psychology and Alchemy* 329-330). *Tattoo*

dyad in its case: The self-divided individual remains a duality predisposed to good and evil alike. In this context, the *dyad* is also the hermaphrodite, "two units regarded as one pair" ("Dyad," [n.], def. 1). See Jung, *Mysterium Coniunctionis* 408: "Adam must have had two faces [...]." *Inmate of Space*

Dying wound none but ourselves with the dart: Cf. "He slew himself with his own dart," an alchemical motto that appears in the "Consilium coniugii," *Ars chemica* (Strasbourg, 1566) 186, and that connects the "motif of wounding" to ritual "killing" and "sacrificial death" (qtd. in Jung, *Mysterium Coniunctionis* 30n161). *Saturn's Gramophone*

Each word's velocity, like light or heat, / Such snow as flies: In "Aphorismi Basiliani" (*Theatrum chemicum*, vol. 4 [Strasbourg, 1659] 327), Nicolaus Niger Happelius indicates that "'a life-force dwells in *Mercurius non vulgaris*, who flies like solid white snow. This is a spirit of the macrocosmic as [well as] of the microcosmic world, upon whom, after the *anima rationalis*, the motion and fluidity of human nature itself depends'" (qtd. in Jung, *Alchemical Studies* 214). Jung remarks that "The snow represents the purified Mercurius in the state of *albedo* (=spirituality); here again matter and spirit are identical." In these lines, as he re-channels the alchemical source, the speaker traces *Each word's velocity* to the momentum of the Holy Spirit. *The Round Chaos*

Echo's orisons: In ancient Greek literature, Echo was the goddess of woods and wild creatures condemned by Hera, the jealous wife of Zeus, "never to use her tongue [...] except to repeat what was said to her." Later, she "so wasted away with longing" for Narcissus, "a scorner of love," that only her voice was left to her (Hamilton, *Mythology* 87-88). Here, Echo's orisons become the soulful yet ironic prayers of a summer evening's "distant antiphon" (l. 12), the latter a plainsong intended for responsive chanting. *The Cheshire of Sense*

Edom (ee-dum): an ancient country of Palestine that has long since been associated with the prophesied Savior. Cf. Isa. 63.2: "'Who is this coming from Edom, / coming from Bozrah, his garments stained red?'" *In the Line of Melchizedek*

Elapid's (ell-uh-pidz) cowl: a holistic image that twines spirit and instinct. The elapid is a venomous snake (e.g., the cobra or the black mamba) with small, erect fangs. However, in a posture of intimidation, it has a hood not unlike that of a monk. See Roland Bauchot, ed., *Snakes: A Natural History* (New York: Sterling, 1994) 41, 165. *Elapid's Cowl*

embers tamped down: smoldering ashes [of the sunset] packed firmly or pounded *down* by a series of blows or taps. The image also suggests the confined force of an explosion ("Tamp" [vt.], defs. 1, 2). *Elapid's Cowl*

embodied ka: in ancient Egyptian religion, the immaterial "life force" attached to the body (Françoise Dunand and Roger Lichtenberg, *Mummies: A Voyage through Eternity*, trans. Ruth Sharman [1991; New York: Discoveries-Abrams, 1994] 42). *Orpheus' Rite*

Embodied the door, emboldened we come: The speaker links salvation to conjugal orgasm—in essence, to the experience of eros, the eternal life force. Cf. not only John 10.9: "'I am the door; anyone who comes into the fold through me shall be safe,'" but also John 14.6: "'I am the way; I am the truth and I am life; no one comes to the Father except by me.'" *The Foliate Pebble*

Embosomed* rebis, *victim round with brawn: In *Symbols of Transformation*, Jung remarks that "Archaic Greek idols, such as were found in large quantities in Aegina," depict God as a human cross, a figure with "an immoderately long head, wing-shaped arms slightly raised, and in front distinct breasts" (265). *God's Folly*

Embrace Him in the trace: See *Aion* 37-38, where Jung notes that "The *imago Dei* imprinted on the soul, not on the body, is [but a trace or vestige,] an image of an image, [as Origen (185-254) reasons,] 'for my soul is not directly the image of God, but is made after the likeness of the former image.' Christ, on the other hand, is the true image of God, after whose likeness our inner man [i.e., the God-image, or *Spirit* of God, that indwells the mind] is made, invisible, incorporeal, incorrupt, and immortal." Here, Jung both quotes and paraphrases excerpts from four of Origen's works: *Contra Celsum*, *In Lucam homiliae*, *De principiis*, and *In Genesim homiliae*. *Citizen of the Cosmos*

encapsuled ba: In this line, the *ba*—in ancient Egyptian mythology, "the equivalent of the soul or the personality"—is contained either in a human body, in an alchemical retort, or in a space capsule. See Dunand and Lichtenberg, *Mummies* 42. *Orpheus' Rite*

Encased diaphany: the "spiritual body" of 1 Cor. 15.42-44: "What is sown in the earth as a perishable thing is raised imperishable. Sown in humiliation, it is raised in glory; sown in weakness, it is raised in power; sown as an animal body, it is raised as a spiritual body." *Orpheus' Rite*

Enclose the loop: either the braided knot of the tail-eating Ouroboros, the serpent or "dragon that devours, fertilizes, begets, slays, and brings itself to life again" (Jung, *Psychology and Alchemy* 372), or the ring or circle of End-time's remnant—Christ's bema-seat assembly—saved and present at "the wedding-supper of the Lamb" (Rev. 19.9). *The Set-Up*

Entelechy's particle: In Aristotelian philosophy, "entelechy" signifies "the actualization of potentiality or of essence" ("Entelechy" [n.], def. 1). Here, the *particle* that conveys this meaning is Christ, the "small piece of the consecrated Host or any of the small Hosts given to lay communicants" ("Particle" [n.], def. 5)—in other words, "the substance of Christ under the sacramental species" (Merton, *The Living Bread* 83). In another reading, the *particle* or speck is also Christ's coheir: the human speaker himself. *Inmate of Space*

Entwining the light: In *Catching the Light*, even as Zajonc asserts that "The lights of nature and mind entwine within the eye and call forth vision" (2), he emphasizes that, "no matter how brilliant the day, if we lack the formative, artistic power of imagination, we become blind, both figuratively and literally. We need a light within as well as daylight for vision [...]" (12). *The Quantum Alice*

***ephemerides* (*ef*-uh-*mer*-uh-*deez*)**: the plural form of "ephemeris"; tables that chart the positions of a celestial body during a given period. *Finite Infinite*

Ephesus' ritual: the resurrection of the body. Some Christians believe that John the Apostle did not die at Ephesus, an ancient Greek city in Asia Minor, but ascended to Heaven like Elijah. See John 21.22: "Jesus said, 'If it should be my will that he [John the Apostle] wait until I come, what is it to you?'" *Orpheus' Rite*

***Eros* (*er*-ahs)**: not only "the [Greek] god of love, son of Aphrodite [...] identified with the Roman god Cupid," but also [in psychoanalysis] "the life instinct, based on the libido, sublimated impulses, and self-preservation" ("Eros" [n.], def. 2). *Jack-o'-Lantern; Saturn's Gramophone; Spacetime's Handkerchief*

Eros' meal: the banquet either of the Life Force or of the God of Love. *Eros' Meal*

Euphrates: one of the four rivers of Paradise. In the doctrine of the Naassenes (Gnostic Christians), the "wonderful water [...] of the Euphrates perfects every nature in its individuality and thus makes man whole too" (Jung, *Aion* 184-85). See also John 4.14, where Jesus converses with the Samaritan woman: "'whoever drinks the water that I shall give him will never suffer thirst any more.'" *A Cup of Water; Orbifold*

Eva's second: Mary, the Mother of God, "coming next after the first [Eve] in order of place or time" ("Second[1]" [n.], def. 1). *Heir Presumptive*

Even as rivers fourfold interweave: in Gen. 2.10-14, the four *rivers* of Eden, their names Pishon, Gihon, Tigris, and Euphrates. *Split-Minded*

Even God's folly proves wiser than men: Cf. 1 Cor. 1.25: "Divine folly is wiser than the wisdom of man [...]." *God's Folly*

Even Simon swerved: In John 18.17-27, the apostle *Simon* Peter, when questioned by his accusers, denies three times that he is a disciple of Jesus. *Servant of Nature*

Eve's gamonymus: balsam, an *elixir vitae* "associated [by the alchemists] with the term 'gamonymus,' which might be rendered 'having the name of matrimony.'" Significantly, Eve, as a stand-in for either Earth or Nature, owns the aetheric substance, since it "is to be found in the human body" (Jung, *Mysterium Coniunctionis* 465). For the orthodox Christian, the true medicament—both *elixir* and *gamonymus*—remains, of course, not only the Holy Eucharist, the living Body and Blood of Christ, for which Mary (the immaculate daughter of Eve) was the first human receptacle; it is also Christ—i.e., the Spirit of Christ—that now indwells and infills His tabernacled coheirs. *Elapid's Cowl*

Eve's mechanic: the English physicist Thomas Young, who "first noted [. . .] the phenomenon of wave interference" in 1803 (Davies, *Other Worlds* 65). Here, the biblical Eve, the archetypal mother of humankind, becomes a surrogate for Gaea, the Greek goddess of the Earth and the precursor of all life. *The Quantum Alice*

Eve's Rabbinic tree: In *Alchemical Studies*, Jung states that "the old Rabbinic idea that the tree of paradise was a man exemplifies man's relationship to the philosophical tree" (337). Thus, in the Book of Enoch, "The tree of knowledge in Genesis" becomes the feminine-maternal "tree of wisdom, whose fruit resembles the grape" (318). See also *Psychology and Alchemy* 256, fig. 131: "Adam as *prima materia*, pierced by the arrow of Mercurius. The *arbor philosophica* is growing out of him." *The Crowned Hermaphrodite*

Exhumed His Spirit: At the tomb of Jesus, both Simon Peter and John ("the one whom Jesus loved") disinterred—i.e., brought to light—not the body of Christ but *His Spirit* instead (John 20.1-9). Thus, later, Jesus "breathed on" the disciples, "saying, 'Receive the Holy Spirit! If you forgive any man's sins, they stand forgiven; if you pronounce them unforgiven, unforgiven they remain'" (John 20.22-23). *God's Folly*

Extended its corpse: As a result of the big bang, the body or cadaver of the exploding universe has expanded, stretched, or spread out ("Extend" [vt.], defs. 2, 5). *God's Folly*

the eyeball is bold: Cf. Zajonc, *Catching the Light* 22: "To know is to have seen, not passively but actively, through the action of the eye's fire, which reaches out to grasp, and so to apprehend the world." In effect, "Sight entails the seer in an essential, formative action of image making or imagination." *Eros' Meal*

Feast of Aphrodite, cauldron all gold / Fastened with rivets: In *Catching the Light*, even as he extols the dynamism of the fearless seer, Zajonc reminds us that, according to the philosopher and poet Empedocles (5th cent. BC), "the divine Aphrodite, goddess of love, fashioned our eyes out of the four Greek elements of earth, water, air, and fire, fitting them together with rivets [i.e., metal pins or bolts] of love. Then, 'as when a man, thinking to make an excursion through the night, prepares a lantern,' lighting it at the brightly blazing hearth fire and fitting it around with glass plates to shield it from the winds, so did Aphrodite kindle the fire of the eye at the primal hearth of the universe, confining it with tissues in the sphere of the eyeball" (20). (In the preceding passage, Zajonc cites *On Nature*, qtd. in Kathleen Freeman, *Ancilla to the Pre-Socratic Philosophers* [Cambridge: Harvard UP, 1983] 60-61, frags. 84-87.) *Eros' Meal*

field of the square inch: In *Alchemical Studies*, Jung defines this mystical concept as "the symbol for that which has extension." Thus, "the central white light" of the Tao "dwells in the 'square inch' or in the face, that is, between the eyes" (25). In other words, the Savior locates His kingship in the mind of each coheir: "a higher spiritual being [. . .] is invisibly born in the individual, a pneumatic body which is to serve as a future dwelling [. . .]" (51-52). See also Gal. 2.20: "I have been crucified with Christ: the life I now live is not my life, but the life which Christ lives in me [. . .]." *Trismegistus' Art*

The fingered Jesus: *Jesus* was not only "informed on" by Judas and "identified as the [. . .] victim" to be killed by Pontius Pilate ("Finger" [vt.], def. 3), but also touched with the finger by "One of the Twelve, [the apostle] Thomas, that is 'the Twin,'" who doubted the resurrection of Jesus until he saw the wound (John 20.27). *Bowknot*

Flock of His pasture: Cf. Ezek. 34.31 (AV): "'And ye my flock, the flock of my pasture, are men'"—in other words, are "'Adam,'" not only the collective Israelites, but also the totalistic First Man (qtd. in Jung, *Mysterium Coniunctionis* 413n199). *Crystal*

a foal, then a mole: The young offspring of a horse and the smaller, burrowing animal draw the speaker to his earthly origins. *Liquid Metal Man*

Foam like the cosmos: The speaker describes "the sponge-like structure of the world canvas" (Davies, *Other Worlds* 96), even as he recalls the birth of Aphrodite, the Greek "Goddess of Love and Beauty," who "is said to have sprung from the foam of the sea" and whose name "was explained as meaning 'the foam-risen'" (Hamilton, *Mythology* 32). *Heterotic*

foetus like a crust: the presence of the eternal Jesus in the bread of the Eucharistic banquet. Merton illuminates this mystery in *The Living Bread*: "The Blessed Eucharist is not a wafer of unleavened bread which somehow contains the substance of the Body of Christ. It is no longer bread. It no longer has the being, or the nature of any material object. The sensible accidents of bread remain, it is true, but they do not inhere in any substance. The Being Who is present is entirely invisible, because Christ in this Sacrament is present only in the manner of a substance" (78). *Apostolates*

Foliate pebble: In *Mysterium Coniunctionis*, Jung explains that the alchemists connected the "inwards of the head" to "the *terra alba foliata* (foliated [i.e., leaflike or layered] white earth), which in this case would be the brain," the so-called "abode of the divine part" (435). Jung adds that the alchemists also connected the "white stone" to Rev. 2.17: "and I will give him a white pebble [. . .] and upon the pebble a new name written, which no one knows except him who receives it" (436n260). In *Thru the Bible with J. Vernon McGee: 1 Corinthians through Revelation*, vol. 5 (Nashville: Nelson, 1983), McGee weighs an interpretation of the latter passage even more bracing than that of the alchemists: "the people of Asia Minor to whom John was writing had a custom of giving to intimate friends a *tessera*, a cube or rectangular block of stone or ivory, with words or symbols engraved on it. It was a secret, private possession of the one who received it. [Thus,] Christ says that He is going to give to each of His own a stone with a new name engraved upon it. I do not believe that it will be a new name for you and me but that it will be a new name for *Him*. I believe that each name will be different because He means something different to each one of us. It will be His personal and intimate name to each of us" (909). *The Foliate Pebble*

> ***foot that He trims***: an image that refers not only to the "immoral" woman's anointing of Christ's feet with myrrh in Luke 7.36-50, but also to the royal finery of the bride that "made herself ready" for the wedding-day of the Lamb in Rev. 19.7-9. Thus, in this poem, the heavenly Father shall either "prepare," or "dress," or array even the speaker, His believer-priest as well as His adopted son ("Trim" [vt.], def. 1). Cf. also the parable of the Prodigal Son in Luke 15.11-24: Having "squandered" his life "in reckless living," the repentant son "set out for his father's house. But while he was still a long way off his father saw him, and his heart went out to him. He ran to meet him, flung his arms around him, and kissed him. The son said, 'Father, I have sinned against God and against you; I am no longer fit to be your son.' But the father said to his servants, 'Quick! Fetch a robe, my best one, and put it on him; put a ring on his finger and shoes on his feet. Bring the fatted calf and kill it, and let us have a feast to celebrate the day. For this son of mine was dead and has come back to life; he was lost and is found.' And the festivities began." In addition, here, the phallic *foot that He trims*, i.e., "clips" or "cuts" ("Trim" [vt.], def. 3), obviously evokes the religious rite of circumcision as "the sign of an internal faith" (John Wijngaards, *Handbook to the Gospels* [Ann Arbor: Servant, 1979], 133). *Crystal*

> ***fractal***: in Mathematics, a never-ending pattern; the subset of a self-similar, "geometrically complicated" space, including such "real-world data" as a cloud, a feather, a galaxy, a leaf, "the distribution of frequencies of light reflected by a flower, the colors emitted by the sun, and the wrinkled surface of the sea during a storm" (Michael Barnsley, *Fractals Everywhere* [San Diego: Academic-Harcourt, 1988] 6, 172-73). *Crystal*

> ***freehold***: a life estate; here, the world retained by God for His own use. *Cinderdust*

> ***From point to pyre***: from the gravitational singularity (a hypothetical point in Spacetime at which matter became infinitely compressed) to the Big Bang (the fiery explosion that marked the origin of the universe). *The Cheshire of Sense*

> ***funnelweb***: the filmy network either of the Milky Way or of the Funnelweb Mygalomorph, a "dangerously poisonous spider" that catches insects "by entangling them in a sheet of silk. The spider hides in a tube in one corner of the sheet." See Herbert W. Levi and Lorna R. Levi, *A Guide to Spiders and Their Kin* (New York: Golden-Western, 1968) 16, 24. *Crystal*; *Galactic Pilgrim*; *Liquid Metal Man*; *The Path of Least Action*

> ***furnace***: here, the mother's womb in which the speaker imagines that he gestates in order to be reborn. See Jung, *Psychology and Alchemy* 347, fig. 184, titled "The three youths in the fiery furnace," where fire symbolizes the divine presence, i.e., "the spirit concealed in matter" (346). *The Path of Least Action*

Gaea's (jee-uhz) cauldron keyholed: The speaker suggests that the expanding big bang cosmos produces—in addition to *soma* (body) and *pneuma* (spirit)—an opening for a key: a vital or essential entity not unlike the soul. Gaea (in Greek mythology, the Goddess of Earth) is viewed here as the Supreme Mother of *all* life. See Baring and Cashford, *The Myth of the Goddess* 304. *Cinderdust*

Galactic hominid, Olduvai's hand: The hyphenate earthling—a two-legged primate veined with stellar essence—is also Nature's artificer or *hand*, "a person regarded as having some special skill or characteristic" ("Hand" [n.], def. V, 2). Olduvai Gorge, a ravine located in northern Tanzania, contains archeological sites teeming with fossils and Paleolithic tools. *The Set-Up*

Galeated: "wearing a helmet" ("Galeated" [adj.], def. 1). *The End of Ourselves*

Galilee's strand: Christ often instructed His followers at Capernaum on the shores of the Sea of Galilee. (See Wilson, *Jesus: The Evidence* 79-89.) Here, *Galilee's strand* also signifies the Savior's DNA. *The Set-Up*

Galumph: "to march or bound along in a self-satisfied, triumphant manner" ("Galumph" [vi.], def.). This intransitive verb, a mix of GAL(LOP) and (TRI)UMPH, was coined by Lewis Carroll for "Jabberwocky" (in *Through the Looking Glass* [1871]) and resuscitated by Lewis Thomas in his twentieth anniversary Op-Ed essay on the first lunar landing, "Beyond the Moon's Horizon—Our Home" (*The New York Times* 15 July 1989, New Eng. ed.): "Then, there were those film clips of the man galumphing across the surface [of the moon], weighed down, but not really at all weighed down, by that huge, bulging uniform, clumsy and incredibly graceful at once, light as a leaf." *The Round Chaos*

Gamonymous* (guh-*mahn*-uh-muss) *His side and then a cloth: In *Alchemical Studies*, Jung defines the Greek term "gamonymus" as "a kind of chymical wedding, [. . .] an indissoluble, hermaphroditic union [of Sol and Luna]" (136). *Gamonymous*, the adjectival form adopted here, alludes to the marriage not only of Adam and Eve at the Creation, but also of Christ and His bride (the Church as well as Mary) at the foot of the Cross. The *cloth* is the seamless tunic of the crucified Christ, a garment "woven in one piece throughout" (John 19.24) and offered to His followers either as an emblem of perfect wholeness or as a wedding gift to His bride. *Citizen of the Cosmos*

***Ge* (*jee*)**: a synonym for Gaea (*jee*-uh) and Gaia (*gay*-uh); the Greek goddess of the earth conceived also as a precursor of life. *The Crowned Hermaphrodite; Finite Infinite; In the Line of Melchizedek; The Power of Life; Saturn's Gramophone*

Gehenna: "a place of torment; hell" ("Gehenna" [n.], defs. 1, 2). *Heterotic*

Gender instantiated, spouses fast: the spiritual hermaphrodite as an expression of the unified and coherent wholeness of the individual. In *Mysterium Coniunctionis*, Jung indicates that "Adam must have had two faces, in accordance with [the Rabbinic] interpretation of Psalm 139.5: 'Thou hast beset me behind and before'

[...]" (408). In *Aion*, Jung adds that "The splitting of the Original Man into husband and wife expresses an act of nascent consciousness; it gives birth to a pair of opposites, thereby making consciousness possible" (204). In other words, "individuation is a 'mysterium coniunctionis,' the self being experienced as a nuptial union of opposite halves [...]" (64). *Citizen of the Cosmos*

ghost like a face, / Suspends in cloud, then roves without a trace: both the Body of Christ present in the Blessed Sacrament and the speaker/astronaut projected as a living symbol of God. *Inmate of Space*

Giaour: in Islam, a non-Muslim and hence an infidel. The word rhymes with "hour." *A Cup of Water*

girdle: "a belt or sash for the waist" ("Girdle" [n.], def. 1), like the snake *girdle* that enfolded Athena's peplos, the loose-fitting tunic that the Greek goddess of wisdom wore and that, in this poem, the Blessed Mother (the "Maria" of line 13) also wears. Significantly, in *The Archetypes and the Collective Unconscious*, Jung indicates that, in medieval, occult philosophy, the Virgin Mary became the Christian counterpart of Athena, since both women—each in her own way a fertility goddess—"knew only spiritual motherhood" (46). *Split-Minded*

glaive: a sword—oftentimes, a broadsword, i.e., one for slashing rather than thrusting. *Heir Presumptive*

Glass and the twain, substantiated, slain, / Hover and haver, suspended in pain: the two—Christ the crucified Redeemer and Mary the Mother of God (here, the surrogate for the Gnostic Sophia)—portrayed in their sufferings as pure form or spirit. See Jung, *Alchemical Studies* 197: Transparent glass "is something like solidified water or air, both of which are synonyms for spirit." Jung's remark in *The Archetypes and the Collective Unconscious* is also pertinent—psychologically, "suspension expresses tense expectation: 'Hover and haver suspended in pain!'" (312). In other words, the smitten Savior and either Mary or Sophia experience "the tension of opposites [that] strives for balance" (235), even as they "linger or wait close by" each other ("Hover" [vi.], def. 2) or "talk foolishly or waste time talking foolishly" ("Haver" [vi.], def. 1). *Living in Curved Space*

glue: gum Arabic, or "blessed" red gum, "the [alchemical] medium between mind and body and the union of both" (Jung, *Psychology and Alchemy* 161, 401). *Tattoo*

goatfoot with his fife: either Pan, "a [merry] god of fields, forests, wild animals, flocks, and shepherds, represented with the legs (and, sometimes, horns and ears) of a goat" ("Pan" [n.], def.); or a satyr, an equally goat-like woodland deity and reveler; or Christ, the archetypal scapegoat, a figure here of self-heated bliss no less than tragic joy. *The Power of Life*

Goblin, pixie, puer (*poo*-ere), thumbling that slight: from the depths and darkness of the earth, "infantile chthonic gods" to whom "wonder-working powers were ascribed" (Jung, *Symbols of Transformation* 126-27). *Orpheus' Rite*

God's imago, hyphenate like a bell: The speaker likens the archetypal Christian coheir—a composite of Spirit, soul, and body—to none other than the alchemical Monocolus, the bell-shaped, one-footed, semi-castrated, androgynous Mercurius, here pictured as twin unipeds that symbolize the union of opposites. See Jung, *Mysterium Coniunctionis* 500n135, 506-07, and also Pls. 4-7. *Tabernacled*

Gold and red and green: in alchemy, the three colors, along with the fourth—the "sapphire blue" of the following line—that "lead to the *lapis*, i.e., the diamond whose prism contains all the hues of the rainbow," a manifestation of wholeness (Jung, *Psychology and Alchemy* 187). *Tattoo*

Golgotha's swain: Christ the Redeemer, "born of a woman, born under the law" (Gal. 4.4), presented here as "a lover or suitor" ("Swain" [n.], def. 3). The erotic implication is deliberate, since the anima—the feminine side of the male psyche—"can be [further] defined as the image or archetype or deposit of all the experiences of man with woman" (Jung, *Alchemical Studies* 40). *Living in Curved Space*

the googolsphere: the universe; an absurdist coinage based on another (root) neologism. Thus, the term "googol" (*goo*-gall), which signifies "the number 1 followed by 100 zeroes" (in short, "any very large number"), derives from the "arbitrary use by E. Kasner (1878-1955), U.S. mathematician, of a child's word"—i.e., "goo" ("Googol" [n.], defs. 1, 2). In regard to the "loopy self-consistency" of the "laws of physics and computable mathematics," see Davies, *The Mind of God* 108: "The fact that the physical world reflects the computational properties of arithmetic has a profound implication." It suggests that, "in a sense, the physical world *is* a computer [...]." *Eros' Meal; The Path of Least Action*

the goose of Hermes: not only the round, long-necked, glass vessel—an alchemical retort—likened to a wild *goose*, but also the chief emblem of *Hermes* Trismegistus (the thrice-great *Hermes*), the mythical founder of alchemy. *A Cup of Water*

Goshen (*go*-shin): an idyllic land of plenty. See Gen. 45.9-10, where Joseph sends a message to his father (Jacob, renamed Israel): "'God has made me lord of all Egypt. Come down to me; do not delay. You shall live in the land of Goshen and be near me, you, your sons and your grandsons, your flocks and herds and all that you have.'" *The Set-Up*

gosling: (*gahz*-ling): "a young goose" as well as "a young and foolish or inexperienced person" ("Gosling" [n.], defs. 1, 2). In *Psychology and Alchemy*, Jung reminds us that the goose is "an *avis Hermetis*," an alchemical retort like the stork or pelican (370n79). *Spacetime's Handkerchief*

Gossamer particles hit on a screen: an allusion to the double-slit (or two-slit) experiment conceived by the English physicist Thomas Young (1773-1829) that demonstrates not only the principle of wave-particle duality, but also the probabilistic nature of quantum matter. As Paul Davies explains in *Other Worlds*, "we know that any individual electron (being a tiny particle) can only pass through just one of the slits [as it travels from its source to a screen], so how does it know about the condition of the other one? In particular, how does it know whether the other is open or closed? It seems that the slit through which the electron does not pass (and which is, by atomic standards, an enormous distance away) has as much influence on the electron's subsequent behaviour as the one it actually passes through. [. . .] Phrased differently, the alternative worlds that could have existed, but did not come to do so, still influence the world that does exist, like the fading grin of the Cheshire cat in Alice's tale" (66-67). *The Quantum Alice*

***grazed my face; / In some farther harmony left my trace*:** In *Space-Time and Beyond*, Toben, "in conversation" with Sarfatti and Wolf, speculates that "The 'ordinary' reality [that] we perceive is not one universe"; on the contrary, "it is the *harmony* of phases of movements of an indefinite number of universes" (26-27). In effect, "We exist in all the universe layers simultaneously." Thus, here, the speaker imagines that, at an interconnecting point in his travels, he met himself. (Michio Kaku wittily reviews such copycat possibilities in *Hyperspace* 94-98.) *Trismegistus' Art*

The Great Chain: "The Great Chain of Being"—an ancient metaphysical principle that postulates a hierarchy of different levels or degrees of being, at the top of which is God. *Hourglass*

Griffin with its paw on the solar wheel: In *The Bestiary of Christ*, Charbonneau-Lassay explains that, during the Middle Ages, "Joining in itself the two natures of eagle and lion, the griffin [was] one of the most satisfactory emblems of Christ's dual nature. [. . .] the eagle foreparts [depicted] Christ's divinity and the lion hindquarters his humanity" (402). However, at an earlier time, the Greeks identified the griffin as "an animal of light." Thus, "An old coin from Smyrna has on one face the head of [the sun-god] Apollo crowned with laurel, and on the reverse side a crouching female griffin with its paw on the solar wheel" (399). *Spinner*

***grinds*:** The speaker assimilates piecemeal the semblances of this world even as he expresses, both within himself and through his poem, the sublimated power of life. The term *grinds* connotes not only the absorption of food and/or ideas, but also—with regard to Mars and Venus—the movement of one's hips in the act of love. *Living in Curved Space*

***Grounded His* rebis; *rooted Him in peat*:** Jesus descended to Earth in order "to found [His spiritual hermaphrodite] on a firm basis"—i.e., on lowly turf or in decaying plant matter ("Ground" [vt.], def. 3). *Trismegistus' Art*

***gyve (jive)*:** a shackle or chain, especially one that fetters the ankles or feet. *Bowknot*

had never hissed: In this line, the echoic verb evokes the image of the healing serpent of Moses, the precursor of the crucified Savior. *The Power of Life*

Had on His pathway sacerdotal (sass-er-dote-ill) dried / The victim at the rack before He died: The speaker alludes to the warmth of *sacerdotal* or "priestly" self-incubation ("Sacerdotal" [adj.], def. 1) and to the heat of "the *ignis gehennalis*, the hell into which Christ descended in order to conquer death as part of his *opus*" (Jung, *Psychology and Alchemy* 339). *Jack-o'-Lantern*

Half teased the die in the pit of my eye: The *die* denotes not only "a small, marked cube used in games of chance" ("Die²" [n.], def. 1), but also "the agony of death," the latter term being an abstract noun coined from the verb ("Die¹" [vi.], def. 2). Likewise, here, the *pit* is at once "a hole or cavity in the ground," i.e., the "abyss" or "pitfall" of Golgotha ("Pit²" [n.], def. 1); the omphalos or navel of the world ("Omphalos" [n.], def. 1); and "the contractile circular opening, apparently black, in the center of the iris of the eye" ("Pupil²" [n.], def.). *Eros' Meal*

the hammer dints: When they despoiled the tree of knowledge, Adam and Eve virtually dented—i.e., dealt a blow to—God's other tree, that of eternal life, and thus lost the gift of immortality that Christ alone could retrieve ("Dint" [vt.], def. 1). See Gen. 3.21-24. *The Set-Up*

hand that leprous lit: In Exod. 4.6-7, after God had instructed Moses to deliver the children of Israel from the bondage of Egypt, He prepared a sign for him (one of several) in order to overcome Moses' reluctance: "the Lord said, 'Put your hand inside the fold of your cloak.' He did so, and when he drew it out the skin was diseased, white as snow. The Lord said, 'Put it back again,' and he did so. When he drew it out this time it was as healthy as the rest of his body." *The Quantum Alice*

harvests scrolls: In *How to Know Higher Worlds*, trans. Christopher Bamford (1961; New York: Anthroposophic P, 1994), Rudolph Steiner asserts that the supreme task of humankind "is to harvest from the mortal world fruits for the immortal" (199). See also *Psychology and Alchemy* 306, where Jung describes a "myth-picture" (fig. 158) titled "Mill of the Host": "The Word, in the form of scrolls, is poured into a mill by the four evangelists, to reappear as the Infant Christ in the chalice" (307). The illustration punctuates a theme germane both to Christianity and to alchemy—that "redemption is a work." *Trismegistus' Art*

hawkmoth: In *The Restless Kingdom: An Exploration of Animal Movement* (New York: Facts on File, 1991), John Cooke explains that "hawkmoths [. . .] are very fast, powerful fliers that sometimes bear a remarkable similarity in both sound and appearance to hummingbirds. Although their wings beat at frequencies of 80 Hz [hertz] or less, they can reach speeds of 35 mph, making them faster than any other insects" (179). *Orpheus' Rite*

healed the blind: At Jerusalem, "Jesus saw a man blind from his birth." In order to display God's power by curing him, the Redeemer "spat on the ground and made a paste with the spittle; he spread it on the man's eyes, and said to him, 'Go and wash in the pool of Siloam.' (The name means 'sent.') The man went away and washed, and when he returned he could see" (John 9.1-7). *An Image of an Image*

Heart of the tincture: In *Pretiosa margarita novella* (1546; *Bibliotheca chemica curiosa*, vol. 2 [Geneva, 1702]) 29-30, Petrus Bonus of Ferrara, a 14th-century alchemist, states that the sublimated body [the secret stone] "'is the heart and tincture [the divine color] of the gold [. . .]. When the stone decomposes to a powder like a man in his grave, God restores to it soul and spirit, and takes away all imperfection; then is that substance [*illa res*] strengthened and improved, as after the resurrection a man becomes stronger and younger than he was before'" (qtd. in Jung, *Psychology and Alchemy* 374). In the latter text, Jung adds that "the first main goal of the process" of alchemical transformation is "the silver or moon condition, which still has to be raised to the sun condition. The *albedo* is, so to speak, the daybreak, but not till the *rubedo* is it sunrise" (231-32). *The Set-Up*

Heaven's Cheshire of sense: here, the unseen Savior. The *Cheshire* is the strange cat that vanishes with a grin in Lewis Carroll's *Alice's Adventures in Wonderland*.
The Cheshire of Sense

Heaven's scarab: In ancient Greek literature, the *scarab* is—like the Gnostic Christ—self-born, bisexual (i.e., hermaphroditic), and unicorned (Jung, *Psychology and Alchemy* 452). *The Set-Up*

Heaven's sudary (*soo*-duh-*ree*): the cloth or napkin with which Saint Veronica wiped the bleeding face of Jesus on the way to Golgotha. The word *sudary* is an alternate form of "sudarium," in ancient Rome, "a cloth for wiping sweat from the face" ("Sudarium" [n.], def.). *Spacetime's Handkerchief*

He basked in His sheen: Cf. Jesus' self-appraisal in John 9.5: "While I am in the world[,] I am the light of the world." *An Image of an Image*

Hecate (*heck*-uh-*tee*): in Greek mythology, a "wild huntress" of the forest as well as "a real spook-goddess of night and phantoms [. . .]. As guardian of the gate of Hades and as the triple-bodied goddess of dogs, she is more or less identical with Cerberus. Thus, in bringing up Cerberus, Heracles [the sun-god that cremates himself] was really bringing the vanquished mother of death to the upper world" (Jung, *Symbols of Transformation* 369). See also a crucial passage in Eph. 4.10: "He who descended is no other than he who ascended far above all heavens, so that he might fill the universe."
Trismegistus' Art

Hecate (*hek*-it) in the ground: The Greek goddess of the moon and Earth also resides in the "underground realm of the dead" ("Hecate" [n.], def.). *Servant of Nature*

Hecate's (*hek*-uh-*teez*) stray: In Jung, *Symbols of Transformation*, the ambivalent Hecate is both "the triple-bodied goddess of dogs" (369) and "the mother of all witchcraft and witches" (370). Today, in popular culture, she is even the mistress of black cats. Thus, here, *Hecate's stray* also alludes to Sir John Tenniel's original black and white illustrations of the Cheshire cat in *Alice's Adventures in Wonderland*. *Inmate of Space*

***He cinctures like a serpent Mary's brain*:** In lieu of a crown, Christ encircles Mary's head with a priestly belt or cord. Its shape—a serpentine coil—is meant to display the chaste and healing nature of the Mother of God. *Living in Curved Space*

***he copulates in boles*:** Like the mandrake, a human being "grows, blossoms, and bears fruit" in order to fulfill his (or her) earthly—i.e., fleshly—nature (Jung, *Alchemical Studies* 291). *Trismegistus' Art*

***He enters His Kingdom through web or mesh, / Veil or curtain*:** The incarnate Christ penetrates both the "spun network" of the cosmos ("Web" [n.], def. 2a) and the "separating screen" of the Holy of Holies ("Veil" [n.], def. 2). Here, of course, the new *curtain* or cover ("Curtain" [n.], def. 2) is "the offering of the body of Jesus Christ once and for all" (Heb. 10.10). These lines also evoke Heb. 9.24: "Christ has entered, not that sanctuary made by men's hands which is only a symbol of the reality, but heaven itself, to appear now before God on our behalf." (In a parallel reading, the pronoun *He* refers to the speaker.) *Inmate of Space*

He has heated Himself with His own heat: In Indian philosophy, through a brooding state of meditation equivalent to self-incubation, "one is fertilized, inspired, regenerated, and reborn." Thus, Prajapati, the unknown creator of all things, practiced *tapas*, a term "to be translated [. . .] as 'he heated himself with his own heat,'" in the sense that, through the heat of libido—of positive psychic energy—Prajapati transformed himself "into something new, into the multiplicity of the world." See *Symbols of Transformation* 380, where Jung quotes Paul Deussen's version of the Rig-Veda (X, 121) in *Allgemeine Geschichte der Philosophie*, vol. I (Leipzig, 1894-1917) 181. *Trismegistus' Art*

He knotted the navel: The speaker refers to the severed thread of the umbilicus, the scar that "remains forever knotted [like a birthmark], right on the body, at the place of the navel." Jacques Derrida analyzes its figurative meaning in *Resistances of Psychoanalysis*, trans. Peggy Kamuf, Pascale-Anne Brault, and Mitchell Naas (1996; Stanford: Stanford UP, 1998) 11. *Tattoo*

Hellas (*hell*-us): "in ancient times, Greece, including the islands & colonies" ("Hellas" [n.], def.). *Finite Infinite*

He mounts the universe: The speaker strives either "to ascend" or "climb" the *chaos confusum*—the primordial chaos; or "to place [a globe or a map of the universe] on something raised"—e.g., on a desk; or "to fix" the whole world as "(a specimen) on (a slide) for microscopic study" ("Mount^2" [vt.], defs. 1, 5, 6b). See also Jung, *Psychology and Alchemy* 133, fig. 64, in which "Christ as Anthropos" straddles "the globe, flanked by the four elements," and 324, fig. 164, in which Mercurius stands "on the round chaos, holding the scales." *The Round Chaos*

Hephaestus (hee-*fes*-tus): in Greek mythology, an artificer—the lame god of fire and metal-working—who is also the husband of Aphrodite (*af*-roh-*dye*-tee), the goddess of love. *Entwining the Light; The Set-Up*

Her bowknot: Gaea's true love-knot, "with two loops and two ends" difficult to untie—hence, a symbol of lasting love ("Bowknot" [n.], def.). *Bowknot*

He rests His tabernacle in its rinse: Christ grounds his "dwelling place" in the blood of the Cross ("Tabernacle" [n.], def. 1b). *The Set-Up*

herm: a rectangular stone post bearing a carved head or bust, originally of Hermes, the Greek god who served as messenger, scribe, and herald for the other gods. *Galactic Pilgrim*

***hermaphrodite* (her-*maf*-roh-*dite*)**: after Hermaphroditus, the son of Hermes and Aphrodite. While bathing, he became united in a single body with the nymph Salmacis. In *The Archetypes and the Collective Unconscious*, Jung suggests that, although "the original hermaphrodite type [. . .] seems to go far back into prehistory" (69n27), in modern psychological parlance, "The hermaphrodite means nothing less than a union of the strongest and most striking opposites. [. . .] As civilization develops, the bisexual primordial being turns into a symbol of the unity of personality, a symbol of the self, where the war of opposites finds peace. In this way the primordial being becomes the distant goal of man's self-development, having been from the very beginning a projection of his unconscious wholeness" (173-75). See also *Mysterium Coniunctionis* 408: In a key passage, Jung indicates that, at the Creation, "Adam must have had two faces, in accordance with [the Rabbinic] interpretation of Psalm 139.5: 'Thou hast beset me behind and before'[. . .]." *Astronaut; The Crowned Hermaphrodite; Hourglass*

Hermaphrodite echoic as a bell: The speaker evokes the *rebis* (from the Latin *res bina*, literally, two-faced matter) as a resonant symbol of wholeness. A picture of the sun-moon *rebis* (*ray*-bis) appears in Jung, *Psychology and Alchemy* 244, fig. 125. The image of the *bell* recalls the chasuble, the priest's outer vestment shaped, originally, like a *bell*. *Astronaut*

Hermes: in Greek mythology, "the god who serves as herald and messenger of the other gods, generally pictured with winged shoes and hat, carrying a caduceus [. . .]" ("Hermes" [n.], def.). His Roman counterpart is Mercury. Significantly, Jung notes that, in alchemical literature, "Hermes or Mercurius possessed a double nature, being a chthonic god of revelation and also the spirit of quicksilver, for which reason he was represented as a hermaphrodite" (*Psychology and Alchemy* 65). *Eros' Meal*

Hermes slips through the narrow: Cf. Matt. 7.13: "'Enter by the narrow gate. The gate is wide that leads to perdition, [. . .] but the gate that leads to life is small and the road is narrow, and those who find it are few.'" The line also echoes John 10.8: "'I am the door; anyone who comes into the fold through me shall be safe.'" Here, of course, the proper noun *Hermes* refers less to the herald of the gods who is also the "guide of departed souls to Hades" ("Hermes" [n.], def.) than it does to the repentant speaker himself. *Eros' Meal*

Hermetic when on the round chaos whirled: Both as spinning astronaut and as floating foetus, the speaker is "derived from Hermes Trismegistus and his lore" and is "completely sealed" ("Hermetic" [adj.], defs. 1, 3). See also the picture of the hermaphroditic infant that springs from *the round chaos* in Jung, *Psychology and Alchemy* 324, fig. 164. *The Round Chaos*

The heron borne on air abrim with sun / Receives in its eyes its rays: In *Symbola aureae mensae duodecim nationum* (Frankfurt on the Main, 1617), Michael Maier mentions that, as a symbol of the godhead, the eagle, being "'fugitive and winged, [. . .] flies up to the clouds and receives the rays of the sun in his eyes'" (192). He adds, however, that "'Were it not for the earth in our work [i.e., the toad] the air would fly away, neither would the fire have its nourishment, nor the water its vessel'" (200; qtd. in Jung, *Mysterium Coniunctionis* 4-5). In this poem, although the *heron* replaces Maier's eagle, the idea remains unchanged: According to Jung, the pair of opposites [*heron*, toad] constitutes "the phenomenology of the paradoxical self: man [and woman's] totality" (6). *Astronaut*

Her skyey scroll: Maya's web likened to the ethereal convolution of a cloud as well as to the rolled parchment of Revelation. *Liquid Metal Man*

He sits like a shade, a man in his booth: Cf. Søren Kierkegaard, *The Sickness unto Death*, trans. Alastair Hannay (1849; Penguin, 1989) 157: "The man sitting in a glass case is not so constrained as is each human being in his transparency before God." *The Cheshire of Sense*

heterotic string: a fundamental component of matter; a closed *string* with two types of vibrations—the clockwise and the counterclockwise—"that [seemingly] live in two different dimensions" of space. "That is why it is named after the Greek word for *heterosis*, which means 'hybrid vigor'" (Kaku, *Hyperspace* 158). *Heterotic*

He vitrifies my helmet: Christ solidifies the transparency of the astronaut's (plastic) bubble helmet. The reference to vitrification—the conversion into glass—is Hermetic. Thus, in *Alchemical Studies*, Jung explains that "For Zosimos [3rd cent. AD] and the later alchemists the head had the meaning of the 'omega element' or 'round element' [. . .], a synonym for the arcane or transformative substance" (72). See also Jung's description of the Philosopher's stone as "'the Chemical King,'" as "'the king descending from Heaven,'" and as "'a tall and helmeted man' (homo galeatus et altus)," in *Mysterium Coniunctionis* 263n21. *Cinderdust*

hierodules (hi-ar-oh-doolz): in ancient Greece, temple slaves "dedicated to the service of a god" ("Hierodule" [n.], def.). *Eros' Meal*

Hierophant at sunrise astride His mare: Cf. John 12.12-15: "The next day the great body of pilgrims who had come to the [Passover] festival, hearing that Jesus was on the way to Jerusalem, took palm branches and went out to meet him, shouting, 'Hosanna! Blessings on him who comes in the name of the Lord! God bless the king of Israel!' Jesus found a donkey and mounted it, in accordance with the text of Scripture: 'Fear no more, daughter of Zion; see, your king is coming, mounted on an ass's colt.'"

Galactic Pilgrim

    hierophants astride / A tower of turtles: Cf. Davies, *The Mind of God* 223: "In his famous book *A Brief History of Time,* Stephen Hawking begins by recounting a story about a woman who interrupts a lecture on the universe to proclaim that she knows better. The world, she declares, is really a flat plate resting on the back of a giant turtle. When asked by the lecturer what the turtle rests on, she replies, 'It's turtles all the way down!'" Davies remarks that "In our quest for ultimate answers it is hard not to be drawn, in one way or another, to the infinite. Whether it is an infinite tower of turtles, an infinity of parallel worlds, an infinite set of mathematical propositions, or an infinite Creator, physical existence surely cannot be rooted in anything finite" (229-30). *The Set-Up*

    ***Hill of Moriah* (moh-*rye*-uh)**: See Gen. 22.1-2: "The time came when God put Abraham to the test. 'Abraham,' he called, and Abraham replied, 'Here I am.' God said, 'Take your son Isaac, your only son, whom you love, and go to the land of Moriah. There you shall offer him as a sacrifice on one of the hills which I will show you.'" *Inmate of Space*

    His cloudform siphoned: Like an alchemist, Jesus drew the divine essence—the true *prima materia* or transforming substance—from His sacred Body and Blood. *Trismegistus' Art*

    His consort* in *the stew: either Eve, the "preformed" spouse of the first Adam (Baring and Cashford, *The Myth of the Goddess* 519), or the Virgin Mary, the "acknowledged" bride of the second Adam (604). Here, the *stew* refers to the cosmic churn. *Tattoo*

    His cross-beam, hoisted, quarters like a clock: Christ—conceived as Cross, quaternity, and/or cosmic clock—completes the map of His own runner's route at Golgotha. Here, as in other poems in this book, the quaternity (the three [i.e., the divine Trinity] + one [i.e., the individual human percipient]) represents totality. This line also contains a hidden alchemical conceit: the squaring of the circle, an apt symbol of the alchemical *opus*, since the latter process "breaks down the original chaotic unity into the four elements and then combines them in a higher unity. Unity is represented by a circle and the four elements by a square." In effect, Christ has taught the speaker that he must be separated from his body in order to be resurrected. See Jung, *Psychology and Alchemy* 124-28, along with the alchemical quip accompanying fig. 59: "'All things do live in the three / But in the four they merry be.'" *Astronaut*

    His dart: Cupid's arrow. See also John 19.34: After the death of Jesus, "one of the soldiers stabbed his side with a lance, and at once there was a flow of blood and water." *Spacetime's Handkerchief*

    His disks, embedded in eclipse: in alchemical literature, a staple conceit, as Jung demonstrates in *Mysterium Coniunctionis*: "the moon, standing on the borders of the sublunary world ruled by evil, has a share not only in the world of light but also in the daemonic world of darkness [. . .]. That is why her changefulness is so significant symbolically: she is duplex and mutable [. . .]" (25). Thus, "the sun in the embrace of the new moon is treacherously slain by the snake-bite [. . .] of the mother-beloved, or pierced by the *telum passionis*, Cupid's arrow. These ideas explain the strange picture in [Hieronymus] Reusner's *Pandora* [1588], showing Christ being pierced with a lance by a crowned virgin whose body ends in a serpent's tail" (30). In other words, "The moment of the [solar] eclipse and mystic marriage is death on the cross" (33). *The Set-Up*

His elixir: not only the water with which John baptized (Matt. 3.11), but also the blood with which Christ saved (Matt. 26.27-29), His believer-priests. In addition, the word *elixir*—a heaven-sent medicament—connotes the lunar or composite water of alchemy, its substance both male and female, i.e., hermaphroditic. See Jung, *Symbols of Transformation* 234-35. *A Cloud in Slow Motion*

His head: Christ perceived as true high priest either in the cenacle at the Last Supper or—as Paul the Apostle describes Him—in "his seat at the right hand of the throne of Majesty in the heavens" (Heb. 8.2). In the same way, Jesus identifies Himself as the head or "main corner-stone" of His Church (Matt. 21.42). See also Jung, *Mysterium Coniunctionis* 513: "in Sabaean alchemy [the head or brain-pan] served as the vessel of transformation." *Citizen of the Cosmos*

His knave: either Satan or the speaker himself. *A Cloud in Slow Motion*

His knoll: Calvary (or Golgotha), the hill outside Jerusalem where Jesus was crucified. *Liquid Metal Man*

His pelican fanned: Charbonneau-Lassay observes that, "On the water," the pelican "has all the grace and elegance of the swan; it is white" and [here, like the (reticulated) python of line 1] "ringed with salmon pink." However, "The European pelican, which entered Christian symbolism as an emblem of Christ, was called *pelekos* by the Greeks, from *pelekus* [i.e., axe], because the opening of its enormous beak, widening out in the shape of a fan, recalls the ancient axe head when the bird drops from the sky onto the fish swimming near the water's surface [. . .]" (*The Bestiary of Christ* 258). *The Set-Up*

His remnant swell: In Rev. 12.17, at the time of the Rapture, "the rest of His offspring"—the true believers—shall ascend to Heaven, but here, according to an ancient myth, in the disc of the moon, "the abode of souls" (Jung, *Symbols of Transformation* 318, fig. 31). *Tabernacled*

His spectre polyglot: Characterizing the Spirit of Christ as *polyglot* or multilingual, the speaker identifies the glorified Savior as the holistic self. Cf. Jung, *The Archetypes and the Collective Unconscious* 357: "The self, though on the one hand simple, is on the other hand an extremely composite thing, a 'conglomerate soul,' to use the Indian expression." *God's Folly*

His spread: not only the spatiotemporal body and blood of Christ—the Incarnate Word—upraised and glorified on the Cross, but also the Mystical Body and Blood of Christ elevated and consecrated in the Holy Sacrifice of the Mass. *Citizen of the Cosmos*

His sprinter's cleat, / Upon the peat, a boson like a beat: The speaker likens the matted sound of a dog running upon a fertilized "plot of ground"—the "lot" of line 3—to the low pitch of a decaying "God Particle," i.e., the Higgs *boson*, the underpinning of the Standard Model of particle physics. See Pallab Ghosh, "God Particle is simulated as sound," *BBC News Science & Environment* 22 June 2010, 5 Aug. 2014 <http://www.bbc.com/news/10385675>. *Elapid's Cowl*

His suit complete: either the deployed astronaut's Shuttle spacesuit or the crucified Savior's "courtship" of humankind ("Suit" [n.], def. 6). Cf. John 19.30: "'It is accomplished.'" *Trismegistus' Art*

His tendrils pending, scale the cargo bay: the NASA astronaut's coiling umbilical tether line compared to the "threadlike part of a climbing plant" ("Tendril" [n.], def.). Here, the "anointed" astronaut floating in the cargo bay of Gemini IV is none other than Christ, an image inspired by the vivid photographs of Edward White's "historic [first] spacewalk" on 3 June 1965, in Kerrod, *Space Walks* (New York: Gallery-Smith, 1985) 18-21. *God's Semaphore*

his token rated, / Cain revenged the gift: See Gen. 4.3-9: "The day came when Cain [the oldest son of Adam and Eve] brought some of the produce of the soil as a gift to the Lord; and Abel brought some of the first-born of his flock, the fat portions of them. The lord received Abel and his gift with favour; but Cain and his gift he did not receive," whereupon "Cain attacked his brother and murdered him." *Servant of Nature*

His wand like a circlet, hook like a mace: an image from an iconic NASA photograph— "Astronaut Bob Stewart [is] attached to the manned maneuvering unit. Near his right elbow are tether hooks to which a variety of objects can be secured. [. . .] The dark wands that curl in front of his helmet are light pipes that signal when the MMU's thrusters are firing" (Allen and Martin, *Entering Space* 112-13). *The Crowned Hermaphrodite*

Horeb: a cloud-covered site—usually identified with Mount Sinai—where Moses received the law from God. See Exod. 24.12: "The Lord said to Moses, 'Come up to me on the mountain, stay there and let me give you the tablets of stone, the law and the commandment, which I have written down that you may teach them.'" *Inmate of Space*

Hosea's claim: i.e., that the Church is the bride of Christ, the all-inclusive, firstborn Son of God. See Hos. 2.20: "'I will betroth you to myself to have and to hold, and you shall know the Lord.'" However, "the greatest turning to God is to take place in the future" (J. Vernon McGee, *Thru the Bible with J. Vernon McGee: Proverbs through Malachi*, vol. 3 [Nashville: Nelson, 1982] 656). *Courtship*

The Host rehearsed: In the Eastern Catholic Churches of the Byzantine rite, the priest cuts the leavened bread crosswise into four sections as a part of the Liturgy of Preparation for the supersubstantial Eucharist. *Navel*

Hourglass yet sutured: Christ configured as a twin-globed glass vessel (both *vas* of distillation and instrument of time) and as a self-born hermaphrodite, being in His human form—i.e., before His crucifixion—not yet self-united. *Liquid Metal Man*

Housel: the Blessed Sacrament administered to Christians. *Heir Presumptive; Liquid Metal Man*

houseled then His dot: Ever since His crucifixion, Christ (in alchemical terms, "a single Monad, uncompounded and indivisible, yet compounded and divisible" nonetheless) has dispensed the Eucharist—Himself—to the human offspring either of the cosmic singularity (Spacetime's own primordial point or *dot*) or of the planet Earth itself (the Voyager 1 space probe's "Pale Blue Dot"). For a succinct analysis of the Monad and the point, see Jung, *Mysterium Coniunctionis* 42-48. *God's Folly*

Hub like a trapdoor: deep space pictured as the silken, tubelike burrow of the *trapdoor* spider. *Orpheus' Rite*

the hub spins by: either the Sun, which the planet Earth orbits once a year, or the central portion of the Milky Way Galaxy, around which our entire solar system revolves once every 225 million years. *Spinner*

hung in the nave: suspended—even as a human cross—in the main part of the interior of a church. See Jung, *Symbols of Transformation* 265, fig. 26. *A Cloud in Slow Motion*

hyacinthine as a bath: In *Psychology and Alchemy*, Jung reminds us that "The coitus of Sol and Luna in the [marriage] bath [of rebirth] is a central mythologem in alchemy, and is celebrated in numerous illustrations" (401n170), including fig. 167: the "Allegory of the psychic union of opposites" (330). *Navel*

Hyacinthine infant: in alchemy, the divine child associated with "The sapphire blue flower of the hermaphrodite" (Jung, *Psychology and Alchemy* 80). *Orpheus' Rite*

Hyacinthine light akin to my size: Cf. John 8.12: "Once again Jesus addressed the people: 'I am the light of the world. No follower of mine shall wander in the dark; he shall have the light of life.'" *Crystal*

hyacinthine master: a reference to the "sapphire blue flower" of alchemy as "birthplace of the *filius philosophorum*" [son of the philosophers] and to the speaker as heavenly adept (Jung, *Psychology and Alchemy* 80, including fig. 30). Elsewhere, in *Aion*, Jung remarks that the *filius philosophorum*, otherwise known as the *lapis*—i.e., the stone, "a *transcendent* unity" (170)—"means nothing other than the self" (127). *The Foliate Pebble*

hyacinthine Prince: Christ in his role as the sapphirine *rebis*. See Jung, *Psychology and Alchemy* 80: "The 'golden flower' of alchemy"—the birthplace of the *filius philosophorum*—"can sometimes be a [sapphire] blue flower," the emblem of the hermaphrodite. *The Set-Up*

Hyaline (high-uh-line): resembling glass, like the Christian Savior and His equally transparent coheirs at End-time. *Bio*

hybrid of the dew: the first Adam, the "true" hermaphroditic microcosm, "who bore his invisible Eve hidden in his body" (Jung, *Psychology and Alchemy* 319n2). In alchemy, the *dew* is but one of innumerable names for the "unknown substance," the *prima materia* (317, 320). *Tattoo*

hyoliths: fossil conical shells found in rocks of the Paleozoic Era (570-245 million years ago). *Bio*

hyperspace: "higher-dimensional space"—according to superstring theory, "the three dimensions of space (length, width, and breadth) and one of time [. . .] extended by six more spatial dimensions" (Kaku, *Hyperspace* vii-viii). *The Path of Least Action; Tattoo*

hyphenate His screen: the weblike cosmic curtain—the very fabric of Spacetime—that separates the phenomenal world from the noumenal. *An Image of an Image*

Hyphenate wean: In this context a noun, *wean* is a contraction of the Scottish phrase *wee ane*, little one— i.e., a "baby": a descendant of Adam and Eve separated from Heaven and connected to Earth ("Wean[2]" [n.], def.). *In the Line of Melchizedek*

Hypnotic the Son had knotted His tail: Christ pictured as the tail-eating Ouroboros, a symbol of divine "self-origination" (Jung, *Mysterium Coniunctionis* 293n138) and concomitant "immortality" (365). See also John 3.14-15: "This Son of Man must be lifted up as the serpent was lifted up by Moses in the wilderness, so that everyone who has faith in him may in him possess eternal life." *Split-Minded*

hypsometric (hip-so-met-rik) atlas: Hypsometry is the measurement of elevation relative to sea level. In *How to Lie with Maps* (Chicago: U of Chicago P, 1991), Mark Monmonier defines *hypsometric* tints as "a series of color-coded elevation symbols ranging from greens to yellows to browns" (24). In this phrase, the *atlas* is both a bound collection of maps and the Titan who supported the heavens either upon his shoulders or with his head and hands. *Liquid Metal Man*

I am His sparks, and I am His limbs: Cf. Christian Knorr von Rosenroth, *Kabbala Denudata*, vol. 2 (Frankfurt, 1684) 248: "'(He [Ezekiel] says [in Ezek. 34.31], as it were, that all the souls of the Israelites were in truth nothing but the first-created Adam.) And you were his sparks and his limbs'" (qtd. in Jung, *Mysterium Coniunctionis* 413). In other words, the Adam Kadmon of the Christian Hebraist Knorr von Rosenroth—"the *homo maximus* [the highest man], who is himself the world" (413n198)—becomes, in this poem, still another [Jungian] reincarnation of Christ—the archetypal "inner man," who represents not only "the totality of the individual," but also "the synthesis of all parts of the psyche," including both "the conscious and the unconscious." Thus, "The 'going out' of the souls from the Primordial Man can be understood as the projection of a psychic integration process: the saving wholeness of the inner man—i.e., the 'Messiah'—cannot come about until all parts of the psyche have been made conscious." Jung adds that this phenomenon may, in fact, explain "why it takes so long for the second Adam to appear" (414). *Crystal*

I am, that I am: an ironic allusion to Exod. 3.13-14: "Then Moses said to God, 'If I go to the Israelites and tell them that the God of their forefathers has sent me to them, and they ask me his name, what shall I say?' God answered, 'I AM; that is who I am. Tell them that I AM has sent you to them.'" *An Image of an Image*

I at my tripod time-lapse the day: At his three-legged stand, [with his camera], the speaker can speed up the day's action in order to comprehend its occurrence. *Elapid's Cowl*

I bear my body as a felon might: Cf. Rom. 8.24: "Miserable creature that I am, who is there to rescue me out of this body doomed to death?" *Tabernacled*

Idaean (eye-dee-an) dactyl: either a giant, like Hercules, or a Tom Thumb, offspring of a race "to whom the mother of the gods [the Greek Cybele] had taught the blacksmith's art" at Mount Ida in Crete (Jung, *Symbols of Transformation* 126-27). *Orpheus' Rite*

I glimpsed the pattern, acted, understood: Having constellated the image of the crowned hermaphrodite, the speaker recognized its carrier (Jesus Christ, the androgynous Son of God) as an archetype of wholeness. See *Psychology and Alchemy* 483: "Experience, not books, is what leads to understanding [. . .]." *Trismegistus' Art*

I have been here before: in effect, the speaker's declaration of his religious faith—I have foreseen or foreknown the events described here. See Jung's comment on *déjà-vu*, precognition, and "meaningful coincidence" in *Synchronicity: An Acausal Connecting Principle*, trans. R. F. C. Hull (1960; Princeton: Princeton UP, 1973) 106-07. *A Cloud in Slow Motion*

I lay in Her lap till I felt the dart: To balance his masculine disposition, the Virgin tamed the speaker either with the lance of Christ or with the arrow of Cupid. Cf. Jung, *Psychology and Alchemy* 438, fig. 241: "Virgin taming a unicorn," where the Virgin Mary soothes the Christ-like unicorn wounded by the hunter. *Trismegistus' Art*

Image tabernacled: The Spirit-centered human body now holds the essence of the Savior, whereas "the Law contains but a shadow, and no true image" (Heb. 10.1). See also Murray, *The Spirit of Christ* 167: "In the Father we have the unseen God, the author of all. In the Son of God revealed, made manifest, and brought near we have the form of God. In the Spirit of God, we have the power of God dwelling in the human body and working in us [. . .]." However, "What the Father has purposed, and the Son has procured, can be appropriated in the Body of Christ [i.e., in the Church and in the individual] only through the active operation of the Holy Spirit." *Inmate of Space*

Impaled the fish with a pole to the bunt: This line presupposes that the earliest Christian believers were fishes, as in Matt. 4.19: "Jesus said to them, 'Come with me, and I will make you fishers of men.' And at once they left their nets and followed him." Jung explores this astrological myth in *Aion* 89-94. *Tattoo*

Implant my furrowed print: In *The Grand Tour: A Traveler's Guide to the Solar System* (New York: Workman, 1981), Ron Miller and William K. Hartmann note that, on 20 July 1969, "Neil Armstrong and Edwin Aldrin, Jr., made the first human footprints on an unearthly landscape, while Michael Collins patiently orbited overhead in the command module. [. . .] they left this monument on the lava plains of Mare Tranquillitatis. Barring accident, it will last for aeons" (120). *Astronaut*

implicate order: a new worldview proposed by David Bohm (1917-1994), a renowned theoretical physicist. In this model of reality—as in a hologram—any element contains, enfolded within itself, the totality of the universe. The adjective *implicate*, a neologism, derives from the Latin term *implicare*, to unite, involve, or entangle. *Saturn's Gramophone*

Imprint of the Spirit, heart's pilaster: the supportive Holy *Spirit* that indwells the heart of each coheir of the Kingdom and that the speaker likens to a reinforced column that projects from a wall. Cf. the idea found in Michael Maier, *De circulo physico quadrato* (Oppenheim, 1616) and paraphrased in Jung, *Psychology and Alchemy* 343: "Little by little the sun has imprinted its image on the earth, and that image is the gold. The sun is the image of God, the heart [as seat of the soul] is the sun's image in man, just as gold is the sun's image in the earth (also called *Deus terrenus*), and God is known in the gold." *The Foliate Pebble*

increased the jar: See John 2.6-9: At the wedding at Cana-in-Galilee, "There were six water-jars standing near, of the kind used for Jewish rites of purification; each held from twenty to thirty gallons. Jesus said to the servants, 'Fill the jars with water,' and they filled them to the brim." Later, the steward at the feast "tasted the water now turned into wine [. . .]." *An Image of an Image*

incubates: The speaker, an Hermetic thinker, obtains spiritual rebirth through the "'brooding' state of meditation." Jung remarks that "In Indian yoga we find the kindred idea of *tapas*, self-incubation," the aim of which is "transformation and resurrection" (*Psychology and Alchemy* 339). *Living in Curved Space*

infinite eight: The hermaphroditic human form, like the number 8, mirrors the shape of an hourglass. According to Jung, the number 8 is a divine multiple of 4 and hence an analogue of the restored Adam and Eve: "we know from experience that the quaternity found at the centre of a [holistic] mandala often becomes 8, 16, 32, or more [paths] when extended to the periphery" (*Psychology and Alchemy* 205). For a useful analysis of the "archetypal numinosity of number," see also Marie-Louise von Franz, *Number and Time*, trans. Andrea Dykes (1970; Evanston: Northwestern UP, 1974) 50-53. *Eros' Meal*

In flickers of light and shadow: The speaker recognizes the split moral condition in which the rarefied astronaut also lives. *The Power of Life*

In liquid silver: in quicksilver, "one of the older [alchemical] symbols for the divine water on account of its silvery-white sheen" (Jung, *Alchemical Studies* 73n24). For the alchemists, water, like air, is synonymous with spirit (197). *Trismegistus' Art*

inmate of space: Sometimes the speaker—a Christian hyphenate of Heaven and Earth—feels like "a person living with others in the same building, [. . .] esp[ecially] one confined in a prison [. . .]" ("Inmate" [n.], def.). However, the epithet also connotes pleasurable, even erotic intimacy, an echo, perhaps, of its root sense: "in" + "mate." In short, finally, the hidden subject of this stanza—the tabernacled speaker himself—embraces the cosmos as the revealed pathway to eternal life. *Inmate of Space*

Inside the lion's carcass combs that swarm: Christ allegorized as mystical food eaten in the Lord's Supper. Cf. Judg. 14.8-9: Samson "turned aside to look at the carcass of the lion, and he saw a swarm of bees in it, and honey. He scraped the honey into his hands [. . .], eating as he went." Here, the word *combs* is a curtailed form of "honeycombs," a framework of six-sided wax cells built by bees to hold their honey. *Apostolates*

In Spacetime, after Yahweh sends the rain; / Encapsules Jesus' atom; like a grain / To Sheol hurtles Him: a recap of the Flood, the Incarnation, and Jesus' descent into Hell, i.e., *Sheol*, in Jewish theology the place of the dead. *Living in Curved Space*

in such dust as dents: i.e., in transitory phenomena—in such "powdery earth or other matter" ("Dust" [n.], def. 1) as empties, lessens, hollows, or depresses. *The Cheshire of Sense*

In the bubble dome: See *The Dome of Eden: A New Solution to the Problem of Creation and Evolution* (Eugene, OR: Cascade-Wipf, 2010) 215, where Stephen H. Webb ponders whether "the earth might be located in a kind of space-time bubble that is particularly void of matter." This dome-like bubble would explain why things look farther away than they really are, "because light is distorted in a void." *Spinner*

In the cubic form of a crystal: See Jung, *Mysterium Coniunctionis* 245: "Salt is not a common dream-symbol, but it does appear in the cubic form of a crystal, which in many patients' drawings represents the centre and hence the self [. . .]." Jung also remarks that, in the Syrian "Book of the Cave of Treasures" (4th cent. AD], Adam's body "'shone like the light of a crystal'" (449). *Crystal*

in the fissure vaster: In *Alchemical Studies*, Jung observes that, according to Paracelsus (1493-1541), in the human skull, "there is an 'aquastric fissure,' in men on the forehead, in women at the back of the head," and that, of all the Paracelsan ideas, "the [celestial] Aquaster [i.e., the quasi-material 'water star'] comes closest to the modern concept of the unconscious" (139-40). The speaker is *in the fissure vaster* because the latter groove relates him telepathically to the spiritual world—even "to phenomena or events indicative of the future" (139n34). *The Foliate Pebble*

In the funnel virtual rotations: In this poem, the *funnel* refers either to the vast spiral disk of the Milky Way Galaxy—its shape determined, at least theoretically, by the torque of the *funnel* of the black hole located at its center (here, a synecdochic image)—or to a light-cone in curved space-time. Concerning the latter phenomenon, in *Space-Time-Matter* (New York: Dover, 1952) 274, Hermann Weyl speculates that, although "'Every world point is the origin of the double-cone of the active future and the passive past,'" and although "'in the special theory of relativity these two portions are separated by an intervening region, it is certainly possible in the present case [general relativity] for the cone of the active future to overlap with that of the passive past; so that, in principle, . . . [I may well] experience events now that will in part be an effect of my future resolves and actions. . . . The result would be a spectral image of the world more fearful than anything [that] the weird fantasy of E. T. A. Hoffmann has ever conjured up'" (qtd. in Toben, "in conversation" with Sarfatti and Wolf, *Space-Time and Beyond* 133). *The Power of Life*

in the leprous light: The word *leprous* is an alchemical epithet—either impure, unclean, contaminated, or corrupt, like "metals, oxides, and salts" (Jung, *Alchemical Studies* 290n6). In this poem, the light is *leprous* because, as Jung suggests in *Mysterium Coniunctionis*, "The changefulness of the moon and her ability to grow dark are interpreted [by the alchemists] as her corruptibility, and this negative quality can even darken the sun" (28). *Crystal*

In the opposite direction facing, / Walking backward along yet still pacing: Cf. Robert Gilmore, *Alice in Quantumland: An Allegory of Quantum Physics* (New York: Copernicus-Springer-Verlag, 1995), where the quantum Alice spotted a figure who "looked somewhat like Alice herself. [. . .] She noted to her surprise that, although the girl was coming toward her, she was facing in the opposite direction and walking along backward" (88). In other words, as Gilmore explains, given the fuzziness of virtual reality, "particles can be in two places at the same time." Apparently, since all particles have their antiparticles, they "can even turn around" (107). Thus, here, going backward in time, Alice runs into herself. *The Quantum Alice*

In the vas of Her moon: the Blessed Mother projected as a moon-goddess—or, "in the Catholic conception of Christ's androgyny," as a symbol of the Savior's "counterbalancing femininity" (Jung, *Aion* 205). *Tabernacled*

in the vessel curled: The speaker compares himself to both an astronaut confined in a space capsule and a foetus coiled in a womb. The image also recalls the *vas Hermeticum* of alchemy, a retort that was "'hermetically' sealed (i.e., sealed with the sign of Hermes); [. . .] had to be made of glass, and had also to be as round as possible, since it was meant to represent the cosmos in which the earth was created" (Jung, *Alchemical Studies* 197). *The Round Chaos*

Invests my astronaut: [Christ] clothes or arrays His new disciple in the symbols of earthly power and heavenly authority. *Cinderdust*

I riffle through Eve's physics: The speaker would "leaf rapidly through" Eve's Book of Life, "as by letting the edges or corners of the pages slip lightly across the thumb" ("Riffle" [vt.], def. 2). *God's Folly*

Iris' (eye-ris) braided ring: not only the rainbow associated with Iris, a Greek goddess, but also "the round, pigmented membrane surrounding the pupil of the eye [. . .]" ("Iris" [n.], def. 2) and, at its periphery, continuous with the muscular ring of hairlike projections called the ciliary body. See Nilsson and Lindberg, *Behold Man* 187. *Saturn's Gramophone*

I rise as I began; not yet a man, / Paraphrase the hyphenate: As a mirror of the androgynous Original Man of Gnosticism, the masculo-feminine speaker himself reifies the archetype of Yahweh's sun-moon hermaphrodite. Here, he is also *hyphenate* because, as a coheir of Christ, he is connected to both Heaven and Earth. See Jung, *Mysterium Coniunctionis* 407-08, along with *Symbols of Transformation* 265, fig. 26. *Living in Curved Space*

the iron swam / On a borrowed stick: not only the swerving car that cracked its brake drum, but also the floating axe head that prefigures the resurrected Christ in 2 Kings 6.1-7. *An Image of an Image*

I run my race: Cf. 1 Tim. 6.12: "Run the great race of faith and take hold of eternal life." *Liquid Metal Man*

Isaac at the altar; priest with his knife: On his journey to Canaan, "when God put Abraham to the test" (Gen. 22.1), the first patriarch and ancestor of the Hebrews "built an altar and arranged the wood. He bound his son Isaac and laid him on the altar on top of the wood. Then he stretched out his hand and took the knife to kill his son [. . .]" (Gen. 22.9-11). *The Power of Life*

I saw an artifex like a vender / Hypnotize a body: the self-transforming alchemist, portrayed as both street-corner magician and Gypsy hypnotist. Here, the adept is drawn *less* to the separation of the sexes than he is to "the indescribable totality" of the Gnostic Adam—i.e., to the hermaphrodite that exists "beyond division by sex" (Jung, *Alchemical Studies* 139). The term *vender*, an alternate spelling of "vendor," upholds the visual pattern of unifying rhymes. *Spacetime's Handkerchief*

I sensed the first path: She curved like a leaf; / Guessed the second: ghost ship or schooner's reef; / Embraced the third as the vassal His fief; / Discerned the fourth, then nudged Him like a thief: The speaker seeks a higher level of consciousness. Thus, as he performs the four functions of consciousness—Sensing, Intuiting, Feeling, and Thinking—he canalizes or converts the instinctual energy of those activities into analogues of salvation. Accordingly, the first path of salvation becomes a body that curves like the single blade of a cloverleaf, the latter's fourfold pattern—whether as plant or as highway interchange—both an overview of the speaker's natal journey and a symbol of wholeness; the second path represents the transit of the souls ferried by Charon across the river Styx to Hades; the third path swerves to Eden, the fief or "heritable land held from a lord in return for service" ("Fief" [n.], def.); and, finally, the fourth path backtracks to Golgotha, the site of the speaker's redemption. The entire venture—a map of the runner's route—is meant to validate Jung's assertion in *The Archetypes and the Collective Unconscious* that, although consciousness can never supersede the totality of the psyche—indeed, consciousness can exist only "through [the human percipient's] continual recognition of the unconscious" (96)—"Every advance, even the smallest along the path of conscious realization, adds that much to the world" (96). *Spacetime's Handkerchief*

Ishtar: in ancient Sumeria, the goddess of love and fertility, a type of the Great Mother linked to the Biblical Eve, Sophia (the Hebrew Hokhmah, or Wisdom), and Mary. See Baring and Cashford, *The Myth of the Goddess* 176. *Finite Infinite*

I squint at the tint; if, by candles charmed, / Should husk the dusk... ?: Zajonc examines this ancient theory of vision in *Catching the Light*. Thus, "The atomists of the Greek world believed that films or images peeled off objects, or were impressed onto the air by them, and streamed to the observer, where they entered the eye. The tiny reflected image of the world that is visible when we look at the dark pupil of our neighbor's eye was taken by them as evidence of these husks" (29). *Entwining the Light*

I stake my stiffened banner: The flag or banner is *stiffened* because "There is no wind on the moon to billow the stars and stripes, so a metal rod had to be extended along the top of the flag to keep it from drooping [...]," as Timothy Ferris explains in *Space Shots: The Beauty of Nature Beyond Earth* (New York: Pantheon, 1984) 126. *Astronaut*

I stepped beyond the base: The first stanza begins as a time-traveller's rumination on the weird topologies of Spacetime. The speaker imagines that he moved beyond matter as the "foundation" or "basis" of life, even as he reached beyond Earth as "a center of operations" ("Base[1]" [n.], defs. 1, 3). *Trismegistus' Art*

I stood on the chaos: the self-transforming speaker as Anthropos, *rebis*, Mercurius, and/or Christ, standing on the globe, i.e., the round *chaos*. See Jung, *Psychology and Alchemy*, figs. 64, 125, 164, and 199. *The Foliate Pebble*

ithyphallic (ith-uh-*fal*-lik) wight (white): a living being with an erect phallus. The phrase evokes the image of the alchemical Hermes, the Greek god of revelation recast as a symbol of the transforming substance. See Jung, *Psychology and Alchemy* 132-34 and fig. 63. *Orpheus' Rite; Servant of Nature*

***I track a figure*:** I pursue the Savior, glimpsed here as person, symbol, and trace. *Liquid Metal Man*

***its features coined*:** The phrase connotes not only the impress of a stylized face on a piece of metal—i.e., on "any of various large units of weight or of money [. . .] used in ancient Greece, Rome, [and] the Middle East"—but also the increase of a God-given talent—i.e., of "any natural ability or power" ("Talent" [n.], defs. 1, 2). Equally pertinent, of course, is the parable of the talents in Matt. 25.14-30. *God's Folly*

***its flower—sapphire blue—*:** The speaker refers to "The sapphire blue flower of the hermaphrodite," a symbol of psychological wholeness (Jung, *Psychology and Alchemy* 80). *Tattoo*

***Its skeleton attached*:** After the fall of Adam and Eve, death became the clause or rider affixed to the contract of life ("Attach" [vt.], def. 4). Cf. Gen. 3.19: "'Dust you are, to dust you shall return.'" *God's Folly*

***It winds and winds / Even as the finger, spun from it, twines*:** a pairing of Tantric doctrine and string theory. See Jung, *The Archetypes and the Collective Unconscious* 356-57: "In *kundalini* Yoga symbolism, Shakti is represented as a snake wound three and a half times round the *lingam*, which is Shiva in the form of a phallus. This image shows the *possibility* of manifestation in space." However, from the splitting of Shiva (the One Existent) and the Shakti (its feminine side) "arises, in a gigantic explosion of energy, the multiplicity of the world." Here, the string coiled round the *finger* is also a commonplace aid to memory—a prod, in fact, to the world-creating "discrimination of opposites" (96), the totalistic goal of self-recollection. *Living in Curved Space*

***I walk upon the moon as round as glass; / Craters everywhere, rock chips that I class*:** a moonscape that paraphrases one of the iconic surface-photographs taken during the Apollo 17 mission on 7 December 1972. Astronaut Harrison "Jack" Schmitt forages "beside a lunar boulder dubbed 'Splitrock' in the Valley of Taurus-Littrow" (Allen and Martin, *Entering Space* 136-37). See also Robin Kerrod, *Space Walks* 44. *Astronaut*

***I wheel before God*:** Cf. *The Sickness unto Death* 156-57, where Kierkegaard emphasizes God's judgment of "only particular individuals." Thus, "The man sitting in a glass case is not so constrained as is each individual in his transparency before God. [. . .] Essentially, everyone arrives at eternity bringing with him the most exact record of every least trifle [that] he has committed or omitted to hand over." *The Round Chaos*

***Jehovah's timepiece*:** "*A pendulum clock that goes forever without the weights running down.* [. . .] *The movement without friction shows that the clock is cosmic, even transcendental* [. . .]" (Jung, *Psychology and Alchemy* 104-05). *Split-Minded*

***Jerusalem's rings*:** either the "everlasting movement in a circle" of Jehovah's cosmic clock, "a *perpetuum mobile*" (Jung, *Psychology and Alchemy* 104-05), or the *rings* or assemblies of Spirit-filled believers—"those who wash their robes clean" (Rev. 22.14)—in the New Jerusalem at End-time. *Split-Minded*

Jesse's tree: a genealogical tree—Christians regard Jesse, the father of King David, as the first ancestor in the lineage of Christ. See Isa. 11.1: "Then a shoot shall grow from the stock of Jesse, and a branch shall spring from his roots." *Bio*

Jesus' horn, lamellicorn its base: a conflation of two images, familiar symbols of Christ—the fabulous, horselike unicorn, "with a single horn growing from the center of its forehead" ("Unicorn" [n.], def. 1), and the one-horned scarab beetle, with its antennae described as *lamellicorn*, i.e., "ending in flattened plates" ("Lamellicorn" [adj.], def. 1). *The Crowned Hermaphrodite*

Jesus knew His target: the figure of Jesus fused with that of Cupid, or Eros. The *target* at which the archer shoots is not only the heart; it is also "a round, flat board [...] marked with concentric circles" ("Target" [n.], def. 2a). In effect, the speaker finds that he must "construct or locate an objective centre—a centre outside" his ego-personality. See Jung, *Psychology and Alchemy* 104-05, along with fig. 48. *Spacetime's Handkerchief*

jinn: in the sea of the unconscious, the spirit in the bottle that the *lapis*—the healing stone correlated with Christ—seeks to liberate and to transform. *Split-Minded*

Jonah hated: *Jonah*, a prophet of God, *hated* the Ninevites; when God commanded him to denounce their "great city" that they might abandon their "wickedness," *Jonah* refused (Jon. 1:1-3). *Servant of Nature*

ken: "mental perception; range of knowledge; [or] understanding" ("Ken" [n.], def. 2). *God's Folly*

Kevlar: a brand name for a heat-resistant, synthetic fiber used in making the outer layer of the Shuttle spacesuit. *Crystal*

King David, baited, / Sacrificed the Hittite: Goaded by his love for Bathsheba, *King David* sent her husband, Uriah *the Hittite*, to certain death on the battlefield. Then, after a period of mourning, he "brought her into his house," and she "became his wife and bore him a son. But what David had done was wrong in the eyes of the Lord" (2 Sam. 11.27). *Servant of Nature*

kite: a predatory bird of the hawk family, "with long, pointed wings and, usually, a forked tail" ("Kite" [n.], def. 1). *Orpheus' Rite*

a kite / Suffused by snow: The speaker conflates two stages of the alchemical process of transformation—specifically, the *nigredo* or blackness, the initial state, and the subsequent "silver or moon condition," the *albedo* or whitening. Here, the *kite* or hawk is a substitute for the raven, a recurrent "*nigredo* symbol." See Jung, *Psychology and Alchemy* 230, fig. 115. *Tabernacled*

A lace and then a face: Christ's imprint on Veronica's sudary. *Citizen of the Cosmos.*

Lachesis' loom: In Greek and Roman mythology, Lachesis (*lack*-uh-sis) measures the thread of life that Clotho (*kloh*-thoh) spins and that Atropos (*at*-roh-*pahs*) cuts. *God's Semaphore*

Lady, like Hephaestus, you make me wince: The *Lady* is Aphrodite, the Goddess of Love caught—along with Ares, her lover—in a chain-link net forged by *Hephaestus*, their cuckold. See Jung's pertinent observation in *Mysterium Coniunctionis* 289: "the regimen of Venus [Aphrodite] leads by implication" to passion as well as to death. *The Set-Up*

lammergeier's wight: the lamblike Christ—a *wight* or living being—pictured as the prey of the satanic lammergeier, the sheep vulture. *The Cheshire of Sense*

Lance to the wafer: At the Breaking of the Sacred Host during the Holy Sacrifice of the Mass, the priest "places one half on the paten and breaks off a particle [the *particula*] from the other," an unbloody rite that reenacts Christ's death on the Cross (*Saint Joseph Daily Missal* 686). *Spacetime's Handkerchief*

***Leaf veins that deliquesce* (*dell*-ee-*kwess*)**: The veins of a leaf divide repeatedly and so "branch into many fine divisions" ("Deliquesce" [vi.], def. 2b). Here, the speaker alludes to the "charming tales" with "a dark background" that Hamilton reviews in *Mythology* 85-91 and that feature Narcissus, Hyacinthus, and Adonis, "young people who, dying in the springtime of life, were fittingly changed into spring flowers [. . .]." Hamilton notes that such myths "give a hint of [. . .] blood sprinkled over the barren land" and of "hateful sacrifice" (89). *Elapid's Cowl*

Leprous as the moon where His soul shall sit: Jung notes that "in Plutarch [c. 46-120] Hermes [god of revelation and guide of souls] sits in the moon and goes round with it (just as Heracles does in the sun)." In essence, the moon is the "receptacle of souls" (*Mysterium Coniunctionis* 140). *Cinderdust*

Leviathan's* (luh-*vye*-uh-thunz) *fins: winglike appendages that extend from, and propel, the evil "monster of the deep"—either the whale, crocodile, or dragon described in Isa. 27.1. *Jack-o'-Lantern*

lexies: in modern semiotics, sections of arbitrarily coded verbal signs that manifest the *langue* (the underlying linguistic system) that permeates a literary text. *God's Semaphore*

Lift out of my side such skein as He ran: The speaker repeats within himself the marriage of Adam and Eve. In *Aion*, Jung explains that, in Gnostic thinking, "The production of the WOMAN" from Christ's side "suggests that he (the Heaven-sent Savior) is interpreted as the second Adam. Bringing forth a woman means that he is playing the role of the Creator-god in Genesis." In effect, Christ "demonstrates his androgyny in a drastic way" (204). The *skein* mentioned here is either "a quantity of yarn or thread wound in a coil," "a sequence of events" ("Skein" [n.], defs. 1a, 3), or a length of magnetic tape. *Living in Curved Space*

Light, being malleable, plies his tools / With rivets of love: Cf. Zajonc, *Catching the Light* 20: According to the philosopher and poet Empedocles (5th cent. BC), "the divine Aphrodite [. . .] fashioned our eyes out of the four Greek elements of earth, water, air, and fire, fitting them together with rivets [i.e., metal pins or bolts] of love." *Entwining the Light*

like a moth: The speaker compares himself to a Sphinx or hawk *moth* that comes, "like the nightmare, in darkness" (Jung, *Symbols of Transformation* 250). To discover the connection between the *moth* and the sun-hero (Christ and—in this poem—the astronaut, the surrogate for Christ in succeeding stanzas), see Jung's chapter on "The Song of the Moth": *like a moth*, the dying sun-god "rises again in rejuvenated splendour to give light to new generations" (*Symbols of Transformation* 109). *A Cloud in Slow Motion*

like cock and hen: Cf. Jung, *Psychology and Alchemy* 330, fig. 167, titled the "Allegory of the psychic union of opposites" and including the following verses: "'O Luna, folded by my embrace, / Be you as strong as I, as fair of face. / O Sol, brightest of all lights known to men, / And yet you need me, as the cock the hen'" [from the *Rosarium philosophorum* (1550)]. *God's Folly*

Like foam in the cavern: The speaker alludes not only to "the sponge-like structure of the world canvas" (Davies, *Other Worlds* 96), but also—as in Plato's Allegory of the Cave—to the shadow reality of its Maker (Davies, *The Mind of God* 35). *Crystal*

Like Hermes Trismegistus: in Greek alchemical history, *Hermes* "the three times great," a personification of the Egyptian god Thoth and the putative author of works on alchemy, astrology, and magic. Here he appears as "the *archetype of the wise old man*, or *of meaning*," and corresponds at the same time to the archetype of the spirit. (See Jung, *The Archetypes and the Collective Unconscious* 37, 374.) The key source for this image is Marcellin Berthelot's inclusion of the following passage from "The Book of Krates" (9th cent. AD) in *La Chimie au moyen age*, vol. 3 (Paris, 1893) 46ff.: "'Then I saw an old man, the handsomest of men, sitting in a chair. He was dressed in white, and was holding in his hand a board from the chair, on which rested a book. [. . .] When I asked who this old man was, I was told: He is Hermes Trismegistus, and the book he has in front of him is one of those which contain the explanation of the secret things he has hidden from men'" (qtd. in Jung, *Psychology and Alchemy* 250n7). See also the depiction of *Hermes* as the man seated on the cathedra in Jung, *Psychology and Alchemy* 249, fig. 128. *The Round Chaos*

Like Mars and Venus, concrete as a thumb: a nod not only to the archetypal pair of opposites—male and female—entwined in the net of Vulcan, but also to the psychological wholeness generated by their union. Here, the phallic *thumb* "represents the libido, or psychic energy in its creative aspect" (Jung, *Symbols of Transformation* 124). *The Foliate Pebble*

Like Mars and Venus implicated: a reference to alchemical transformation as well as to sexual consummation. In *Mysterium Coniunctionis* 288-89, Jung states that, in the procedure called the regimen of *Venus*, "the color changes into a livid purple, whereupon the philosophical tree will blossom. Then follows the regimen of Mars, 'which displays the ephemeral colours of the rainbow and the peacock at their most glorious.' In 'these days' the 'hyacinthine colour' appears, i.e., blue." (Jung quotes here from *The Hermetic Museum Restored and Enlarged*, trans. Edward Arthur Waite, vol. 1 [London, 1893] 694.) In this stanza, of course, *Mars and Venus* are also the lovers "implicated"—i.e., connected with a crime and entangled—in the net of Vulcan ("Implicate" [vt.], defs. 1a, 3). *Living in Curved Space*

Like Solomon himself, I cannot speak: The "alien" of the first stanza imagines that, when King *Solomon* met the Queen of Sheba, he was overcome by her generosity—"Never again came such a quantity of spices as the queen of Sheba gave to King Solomon" (1 Kings 10.10). *The End of Ourselves*

Like the eye of some cat with paws that clang: the *eye* of the vanishing Cheshire *cat* from Lewis Carroll's *Alice's Adventures in Wonderland* taken here as a symbol of the fiery explosion that occurred at the birth of the Universe. The *paws that clang* refer not only to the "static noise"—the radiation left over—from the primordial fireball, but also to the clamorous trumpet of the seventh angel at End-time (Rev. 11.15). *Spinner*

Like us he is not alone in the night: In "When Galaxies Collide," Sharon Begley reasons that, according to images captured by the Hubble Space Telescope, "it is a rare star that does not eventually have planets. Which makes the odds that we are not alone in the universe even shorter" (*Newsweek* 2 Nov. 1997: 3, 23 June 2014 <http://www.newsweek.com/when-galaxies-collide-171246>). *Courtship*

Limpets: any of numerous marine gastropod molluscs "with a single, low, cone-shaped shell and a thick, fleshy foot, by means of which it clings to rocks, timbers," and ships' hulls ("Limpet" [n.], def.). In line 7, the Slipper Limpet is so-called because, when the sea snail is turned upside down, a section of its shell resembles the arched surface or "deck" of a slipper. *Heterotic*

Lolled exanimate: During his psychic awakening—i.e., his conscious recognition of Christ as both personal and suprapersonal Center—the speaker would "lean or lounge about in a relaxed or lazy manner" ("Loll" [vi.], def. 1) or, alternately, in a "dead" or "inert" or "spiritless" condition ("Exanimate" [adj.], defs. 1, 2). *Trismegistus' Art*

loller in heat: a sexually excited dog that lingers lazily. *Elapid's Cowl*

magic slough like kale: two symbols of continuous creation that intersect—the dead outer skin shed periodically by a serpent and the harvest of leaves produced from

Black Magic Kale, a plant of the crucifer family. *Split-Minded*

mandrake: the root of the mandragora, a medicinal plant, formerly thought to possess occult powers because of its supposed resemblance to the human body—specifically, to a man standing upside down. In *Alchemical Studies*, Jung notes that "The idea that man is an inverted tree seems to have been current in the Middle Ages. [...] In Hindu literature the tree grows from above downwards, whereas in alchemy (at least according to the pictures) it grows from below upwards." However, "In East and West alike, the tree symbolizes a living process as well as a process of enlightenment" (312-14)—in fine, the work of both "[moral] transformation and [spiritual] renewal" (317). See also *Carrying the Fire: An Astronaut's Journey* (1974; New York: Ballantine-Random, 1975) 371, where Michael Collins describes his own "inverted tree" scene from the Apollo 11 expedition: "The world outside my window is breathtaking; in the three short years since Gemini 10, I have forgotten how beautiful it is, as clouds and sea slide majestically and silently by. We are [lying in individual couches] 'upside down,' in that our heads are pointed down toward the earth and our feet toward the black sky, and this is the position in which we will remain for the next two and a half hours in earth orbit, as we prepare ourselves and our machine for the next big step, the translunar injection burn which will propel us toward the moon. The reason for the heads-down attitude is to allow the sextant, in the belly of the C[ommand] M[odule], to point up at the stars, for one of the most important things I must do is [to] take a couple of star sightings to make sure that our guidance and navigation equipment is working properly before we decide to take the plunge and leave our safe earth orbit." *Bio; Trismegistus' Art*

manna: the food given by God to the Israelites during the exodus from Egypt: "Israel called the food manna; it was white, like coriander seed, and it tasted like a wafer made with honey" (Exod. 16.31). *Elapid's Cowl; The Set-Up; Trismegistus' Art*

Maria's twelves: In *The Archetypes and the Collective Unconscious*, Jung explains the meaning of "the number 12," even as he clarifies the individuation process in its relation to astrological symbolism. Thus, "Twelve is four times three," a reconfiguration of the axiom of Maria Prophetissa, "that peculiar dilemma of three and four [...]. I would hazard that we have to do here with a *tetrameria* (as in Greek alchemy), a transformation process divided into four stages of three parts each, analogous to the twelve transformations of the zodiac and its division into four. As not infrequently happens, the number 12 would then have a not merely individual significance [as one's birth number, for instance], but a time-conditioned one too, since the present aeon of the Fishes is drawing to its end and is at the same time the twelfth house of the zodiac" (310). In short, as Jung also indicates in *Mysterium Coniunctionis*, since the soul "was imprinted with a horoscopic character at the time of its descent into birth," the journey of each mystic traveller through the planetary houses "boils down to becoming conscious" now of one's "godlikeness" (231). *The End of Ourselves*

Marry the goatfoot that leaps from my pen: The speaker longs to unite the absolute opposites that determine his identity—his "inner, eternal man" with his "outer, mortal man." (See Jung, *Psychology and Alchemy* 150.) Here, the *goatfoot* is Pan, the "merry" shepherds' god (Hamilton, *Mythology* 40), while the *pen* is either "a small yard or enclosure for domestic animals" ("Pen¹" [n.], def. 1) or "an instrument for writing" ("Pen²" [n.], def. 4a). *God's Folly*

Mary with her moon-eye: The Christian speaker appropriates an ancient Egyptian myth: "In the autumn equinox the heavenly cow with the moon-eye, Isis, receives the seed that begets Horus (the moon being the guardian of the seed). The 'eye' evidently stands for the female genitals [. . .]." In other words, "the great god [Christ as well as Horus] becomes a child again: he enters into the mother's womb for self-renewal" (Jung, *Symbols of Transformation* 268). *Eros' Meal*

Matrix of the Aeons: the cosmic Anthropos (the Son of Man), "who not only begets, but himself is, the world." The Gnostics "constantly endeavoured to give visible form and a suitable conceptual dress to this being [. . .]." Thus, He is also the "undivided point," the "grain of mustard seed" that grows into the kingdom of God; the "utterance of God"; and the "shepherd of white stars"—in short, archetypal expression as well as eternal source of the unfolding ages (Jung, *Aion* 198-99). *Hourglass*

Maya (*my*-uh): in Hinduism, the illusory world of matter personified as a woman. *The Crowned Hermaphrodite; Jack-o'-Lantern; Liquid Metal Man*

Melchizedek (mel-*kiz*-uh-*deck*): in Gen. 14.18-20, the high priest and king of Salem who prepared a ritual meal of bread and wine for Abraham. See also Ps. 110.4: "The Lord has sworn and will not change his purpose: 'You are a priest for ever, in the succession of Melchizedek.'" *In the Line of Melchizedek*

mell: "to mingle; [to] mix" ("Mell" [vi.], def. 1). *Astronaut*

Mephistopheles' (*mef*-uh-*stah*-fuh-leez) *pup*: "the poodle in [Goethe's] *Faust* out of whom Mephistopheles emerges as the familiar [or guiding spirit] of Faust the alchemist," a "motif" that Jung explores in *Mysterium Coniunctionis* 149. Jung notes that "The Gnostic parallel *Logos/canis* is reflected in the Christian one, *Christus/canis* [. . .]," i.e., Christ symbolized as watchdog of His flock (146-47n280). *Liquid Metal Man*

meson (*mee*-sahn): a sub-atomic particle; a type of boson first observed in cosmic rays. *Entwining the Light*

Metabolized in us: Cf. Saint Bonaventure's explanation of this divine mystery: "'just as no body can live without taking into itself food which agrees with it, so too there is no life for the rational soul except by eating and taking to itself this spiritual food [the Eucharist—the consecrated bread and wine] which is what it needs'" (qtd. in Merton, *The Living Bread* 153). *Bowknot*

Migrant yet hyphenated: the astronaut construed as a sojourner belonging to both Heaven and Earth. *Citizen of the Cosmos*

millipedes: crawling arthropods with multiple body segments and pairs of legs, often found under rocks or logs or in forest litter. *The Cheshire of Sense*

Mind His commandment: See John 13.34-35: "'I give you a new commandment: love one another; as I have loved you, so you are to love one another. If there is this love among you, then all will know that you are my disciples.'" *God's Folly*

Mirror of Ares: The speaker compares the androgynous God-man not only to Aphrodite, the Greek Goddess of Love, but also to *Ares*, the Greek God of War, portrayed here as the paragon of masculinity. *Heterotic*

Mithras with his upcurved lance: In *The Penguin Dictionary of Symbols*, trans. John Buchanan-Brown (1969; New York: Penguin, 1996), Jean Chevalier and Alain Gheerbrant note that *Mithras*, "the savior god of the mystery religions," was often "depicted [. . .] as a hero cutting the throat of a bull" with a sacred spear, here *upcurved* because, having sprinkled themselves with the blood of the bull, the devotees of *Mithras* were "reborn to eternal life" (662). Of course, as these authors emphasize elsewhere, "In Grail-legends, the drops of blood which flowed from the upright spear and were collected in the chalice, express the same idea. This spear was the one which the centurion Longinus thrust into Christ's side" (901). *Spinner*

Möbius' (*mer*-be-us) *run*: one of the many strange topologies of hyperspace— a continuous, one-sided geometric surface "created by twisting a strip of paper 180 degrees and then gluing the ends together." In effect, "outside and inside are identical" (Kaku, *Hyperspace* 60-61). The "Möbius strip" is named after its deviser, the nineteenth-century German mathematician A.F. Möbius. *Bowknot; Hourglass*

Monad: not only the indivisible point—"the jot of the iota"—viewed as a Gnostic emblem of the totalistic man or woman (Jung, *Aion* 218), but also a basic unit of matter—a microcosm—that, according to the German philosopher and mathematician Gottfried Wilhem von Leibnitz (1646-1716), mirrors the universe. *Tabernacled*

Moonplant: In alchemy, "the moon itself is a plant" (Jung, *Mysterium Coniunctionis* 132). Thus, in the alchemical pictures, sometimes the prototype of the tree of paradise is "hung not with apples but with sun-and-moon fruit" (Jung, *Alchemical Studies* 302-03). *Orpheus' Rite*

mottle / Jesus' coheir: [We] "mark with blotches, streaks, and spots of different colors or shades" either Jesus or His tabernacled *coheir* ("Mottle" [vt.], def.). *The Power of Life*

multiverse: a concept that derives from a cosmological theory advanced in 1957 by Hugh Everett, and later by Bryce DeWitt, both of whom argue that an infinite number of possible universes (including myriad copies of our local world) comprises but one part of physical reality (Kaku, *Hyperspace* 262-64). *God's Semaphore*

My One, my True / Aphrodisiac: the Blessed Eucharist compared to a love feast that arouses the senses of sight, touch, smell, and hearing. Cf. "The Bugler's First Communion" in *Selected Poems of Gerard Manley Hopkins*, ed. James Reeves (1953; London: Heinemann, 1961) 41: "O now well work that sealing sacred ointment! / O for now charms, arms, what bans off bad / And locks love ever in a lad!" *Tabernacled*

myrtle: a plant associated with Aphrodite, the Greek goddess of love and beauty. It has "evergreen leaves, white or pinkish flowers, and dark, fragrant berries" ("Myrtle[1]" [n.], def. 1). *The Set-Up*

My sutured astronaut: not just the (physically) hyphenated *astronaut*, but also the *lapis*—the living or animate stone—as the symbolic counterpart of the self. For a pertinent description of the astronaut's spacesuit, see Kerry Mark Joels, Gregory P. Kennedy, and David Larkin, *The Space Shuttle Operator's Manual* (New York: Ballantine, 1982) 3.9: "the [Shuttle] spacesuit (more properly referred to as the extravehicular mobility unit, or EMU) [. . .] consists of three assemblies: the upper torso, the lower torso or trousers, and the portable life system. The upper torso and trousers separate into two units. A connecting ring around the waist joins them [. . .]." In other words, without that metal ring, physical self-division would result. Likewise, in the *lapis*, "the opposites are so to speak united," as Jung shows in *Aion*, "but with a visible seam or suture as in the symbol of the hermaphrodite." However, in the higher Adam, "the opposition is invisible" (247-48). In short, "The union of opposites in the stone [good, evil; consciousness, unconsciousness; male, female] is possible only when the adept has become One himself" (170). *A Cloud in Slow Motion*

Nebo (knee-boh): the mountain from which Moses saw "the whole land," i.e., the Promised Land (Deut. 34.1). *Borderline Noun*

Neither male nor female nor rebis name: Cf. Gal. 3.28: "There is no such thing as Jew and Greek, slave and freeman, male and female; for you are all one person in Christ Jesus." In alchemy, the *rebis* is an androgyne, the "dual being born of the alchemical union of opposites" (masculine/feminine) and recognized "as a symbol of the self" (Jung, *Aion* 268). *Courtship*

nematode trussed: a pinworm, its elongated body either curved, coiled, or tied. *The Foliate Pebble*

Noctuid (knock-choo-id) moths: night-flying *moths* with cryptic coloration that matches their habitat and that enables them to elude detection. *Bio; The Cheshire of Sense*

Nor risen from her krater through its mist: Here, the *krater* is at once "an ancient Greek jar with a broad body, a wide neck, and two handles, used for mixing water and wine" ("Krater" [n.], def.); "a bowl-shaped cavity [. . .] on the surface of the moon" ("Crater" [n.], def. 2); an alchemical vessel; and the womb itself. The mist-obscuring scene recalls the cloud of smoke that emanates from the *vas* of Maria Prophetissa in Jung, *Psychology and Alchemy* 160, fig. 78. *The Power of Life*

the Noun that He bade: the first as well as the second Adam that Yahweh summoned into being. Here, the speaker may also refer to the prophesied return of Christ at the Last Judgment. *Elapid's Cowl*

Numbered are we: In Luke 12.7, Christ says that none of us shall be overlooked by God—"'even the hairs of your head have all been counted.'" *Elapid's Cowl*

nuptial flight: not only the mating-flight of the bees, but also the marriage—to "indestructible life" itself—of the "souls that pass to earth." As Baring and Cashford point out in *The Myth of the Goddess*, in ancient Crete "A bull was sacrificed with the rising of the star Sirius [at the solstice], and the bees were seen as the resurrected form of the dead bull and also as the souls of the dead" (118-19). *Elapid's Cowl*

Omphale's (ahm-fuh-leez) thorn: In Greek mythology, Omphale is "a queen of Lydia in whose service Hercules, dressed as a woman, does womanly tasks for three years to appease the gods" ("Omphale" [n.], def.). Hercules, portrayed here as the vexing *thorn* in *Omphale's* side, had slain the son of a king. *The End of Ourselves*

Ophir's (oh-furz) land: a region rich in gold. See 1 Kings 9.27-28. *The Set-Up*

Orb-web's crucifer: both Christ and the descendants of Adam flung into the "nether regions" of matter (Jung, *Psychology and Alchemy* 304), an orb-weaver's web of fate, even as they carry the Savior's "four-armed cross" (35). *Borderline Noun*

Orion worn / Even as a belt: in Greek mythology, a hunter whom Artemis loves but accidentally kills. "After his death he was placed in heaven as a constellation" (Hamilton, *Mythology* 297). See also Engelbrektson, *Stars, Planets, and Galaxies* 24: "Orion [. . .] consists of seven bright stars that outline the figure," three of which "represent his belt." *The End of Ourselves*

Orpheus' (or-fee-us) rite: self-sacrifice that leads to redemption. Orpheus, the legendary Greek poet-musician, "took the fearsome journey to the underworld" (Hamilton, *Mythology* 104). *Orpheus' Rite*

Our Father's treasure, sifted contraband: in Exod. 16.19, the refined, "weighed," and "scattered" manna that God bestowed upon the Israelites during the exodus from Egypt ("Sift" [vt.], defs. 1, 2, 3). *The Set-Up*

Our Lord's salvific staff: in Num. 21.9, the fiery serpent-staff that Moses erected and that prefigured the saving power of the Cross. *Spinner*

Ouroboros (oar-oh-boar-ahs): the snake that bites its own tail—in alchemy, not only a self-described circle, the *opus* that "proceeds from the one and leads back to the one" (Jung, *Psychology and Alchemy* 293 and fig. 147), but also a symbol of totality. *Borderline Noun; Eros' Meal; Living in Curved Space*

Ouroboros' bait: the crucified Christ projected as the *bait* or lure that captures the Leviathan, a satanic creature metamorphosed here into a serpent. See the matching illustration in Jung, *Psychology and Alchemy* 77, fig. 28. *Eros' Meal*

Our Savior's manna, sun and moon trepanned: the Eucharist, the divine substance *trepanned*, i.e., trephined or extracted—like the archetype of wholeness itself—from the skull of the tabernacled percipient ("Trepan[1]" [vt.], def. 1). In this stanza, the speaker caps a phenomenological overview of human history, not inappropriately, with the interlinked figures of Sol and Luna. *The Set-Up*

Outside the cavern: In many cultures, although the *cavern* is a recurrent symbol of the world, "The characteristic 'centrality' of the cavern [also] makes it a place of birth and of regeneration"—in effect, a "womb" or "passageway" not unlike the cave where Jesus was born and where he was also buried. (See Chevalier and Gheerbrant, *The Penguin Dictionary of Symbols* 170-71). *The Quantum Alice*

Pale blue sapphire of the hermaphrodite: the *lapis*, or sapphire stone—the "transforming substance"—of alchemy. In *Alchemical Studies*, Jung mentions that "The special virtue of the sapphire is that it endows its wearer with chastity, piety, and constancy." In addition, "It was used as a medicament for 'comforting the heart'" (258-59). See also Jung, *Psychology and Alchemy* 80, including fig. 30: "the 'golden flower of alchemy' [. . .] can sometimes be a blue flower: 'The sapphire blue flower of the hermaphrodite.'" *Crystal*

the Paraclete: in the New Testament, "the Holy Spirit considered as comforter, intercessor, or advocate" ("Paraclete" [n.], def.). *Bowknot*

parallel Flatland shorn: a two-dimensional version of Spacetime stripped of its primordial symmetry and companioned by our three-dimensional world. The name of the Big Bang's ghostly remnant derives from *Flatland: A Romance of Many Dimensions*, a novella written and illustrated by Edwin Abbott Abbot and published in 1884. *The Cheshire of Sense*

Parallel sand dunes: See the photograph in Kelly, ed., *The Home Planet* 83 and the related endnote: From Earth orbit, "Southwestern Algeria's Erg Chech shows long lines of parallel sand dunes called siefs. The Erg (sand desert) is in a remote area [. . .] of harsh desert, uninhabited and rarely visited. These parallel sand dunes are about 100 miles in length and 5 to 10 miles apart and are found in very few areas of the Earth. Most sand dunes are transverse sand dunes, or perpendicular to the general direction of the wind." *Inmate of Space*

paraselenae (*par*-uh-suh-*lee*-knee): the plural form of "paraselene"; counterfeit moons—optical illusions that occur when moonlight passes through ice crystals in the upper atmosphere. See also various alchemical interpretations of moonlight in Jung, *Mysterium Coniunctionis* 492n117. Evidently, for the alchemists, the source of the *paraselenae*—the moon itself—contains the "Dew [that] wakens the dead and [that] is the food of the holy." *Elapid's Cowl*

***parsecs*:** A parsec (*par*[allax] + *sec*[ond]) is a unit of astronomical length equivalent to 3.26 light years or to 206,265 times the distance from the earth to the sun ("Parsec" [n.], def.). *Courtship*

***Partake of my prey*:** The speaker feeds on Christ's photographic likeness in the Turin Shroud and on His Mystical Body in the Eucharistic Host. *Liquid Metal Man*

***particulate or crumb*:** a very minute particle of the Eucharistic Host. In *Psychology and Western Religion*, trans. R. F. C. Hull (Princeton: Princeton UP, 1984), C. G. Jung notes that, at the Holy Sacrifice of the Mass, after the Host is split in two over the chalice, a "small piece, the *particula*, is broken off from the left half [...]. The sign of the cross is made over the chalice with the *particula*, and then the priest drops it into the wine" (115). In effect, "the body, or *particula*, is steeped in wine, symbolizing spirit, and this amounts to a glorification of the body. Hence the justification for regarding the *commixtio* [the mingling of the bread and wine] as a symbol of the resurrection" (116). *The Foliate Pebble*

***patent in the scan*:** the archetypal Self secured as privilege, right, or license ("Patent" [n.], defs. 1,4) and recorded as data on magnetic tape. *Living in Curved Space*

***path and sky converge*:** In *Psychology and Alchemy*, Jung considers that "The self is made manifest in the opposites and in the conflict between them" and that "the way to the self begins with conflict" (186). Here, the union of upper and lower suggests that the speaker desires the same wholeness experienced by the "unitary being who existed before man and [who] at the same time represents man's goal" (162). *Elapid's Cowl*

the path of least action: Bob Toben, "in conversation" with the physicists Jack Sarfatti and Fred Wolf, defines this mind-altering concept in *Space-Time and Beyond*. Thus, *the path of least action* is "'ordinary' reality" fixed and patterned according to Newtonian physics. However, another view—that of quantum mechanics—suggests that, since reality is a function of our "participation with an indefinite number" of probabilistic paths (95), we may extend the "infinite lattice" of *least action* strands that constitute our perception of the cosmos, even as we expand our consciousness. In other words, the search for holistic order in the universe can lead us, through "star-like acts of awareness," from one *path of least action* to another (159). *The Path of Least Action*

***peacock*:** "an early Christian symbol for the Redeemer" (Jung, *Psychology and Alchemy* 419), since its "combination of all colors" signifies wholeness (223). *Bowknot; Hourglass*

***pelican*:** either the large, web-footed bird with a long, straight bill (a symbol of the salvific Christ) or—because of its resemblance to the *pelican*—an alchemical retort, the philosophical vessel also called, along with the goose and the stork, "the bird of Hermes [Trismegistus]." See Jung, *Psychology and Alchemy* 370n79. *Borderline Noun; Jack-o'-Lantern; The Set-Up*

***A perfect circle even as a coin / Seamless on its track*:** Here, the geometrical figure symbolizes "the supraordinate personality" of "the total man, i.e., man as he really is, not as he appears to himself" (Jung, *The Archetypes and the Collective Unconscious* 186). See also the parable of the five talents (Matt. 25.14-30) and that of the ten gold coins (Luke 19.11-27). *A Cloud in Slow Motion*

Petition Heaven's lap: The speaker implores either "Holy Mary, [the] Mother of God" to "pray for us," as in the "Hail Mary," a traditional Catholic prayer; or the "'Spinning Woman'—Maya, [here, an enveloping mother] who creates illusion by her dancing" (Jung, *Aion* 11); or, simply enough, even the sheltering sky itself. See *Symbols of Transformation* 268, where Jung quotes a passage from an Egyptian hymn: "Thy mother, the sky, / Stretches forth her arms to thee." *Spinner*

Phaëthon's (*fay*-uh-*thahnz*) braid: the serpentine path of the sun. In Greek mythology, Phaëthon is not only a son of Helios, the sun god, but also an emblem of fatal risk-taking; thus, when the reckless youth drove his father's sun chariot across the sky and almost set fire to the world, Zeus struck him down with a thunderbolt. *Hourglass*

phantom like a bole: the insubstantial Christ reified as both human Cross and Tree of Life. *Liquid Metal Man*

Pinned down: either held fast (by Spacetime or by Maya) or forced to give firm opinions. *Liquid Metal Man*

pintered: a reference to the sparse, foreboding style of the British playwright Harold Pinter (1930-2008). Hence, in this poem, *pintered* (both a pun and a neologism) is the past participial form of the transitive verb "pinter": to imbue [the "bleak and blighted skyscape" of line 6] with equivocal silences, harrowing mystery, and hidden menace. *The Quantum Alice*

plantigrade: "walking on the whole sole, as a human or bear" ("Plantigrade" [adj.], def.). *Liquid Metal Man*

pleasure like a bleat / Attached to the unit, [we] melt as we meet: The speaker expresses his regard for the Shuttle spacesuit even as he dons it. See Joels, Kennedy, and Larkin, *The Space Shuttle Operator's Manual* 3.9: "The upper torso and trousers separate into two units. A connecting ring around the waist joins them, eliminating the need for any zippers in the suit." (The quoted lines from the poem also contain a phallic pun.) *Tattoo*

Plumb bob in the membrane: i.e., a *mental* "plumb bob," or conical metal weight, that, according to the cognitive scientist Steven Pinker, "comes from the vestibular system of the inner ear, a labyrinth of chambers that includes three semicircular canals oriented at right angles to each other. [. . .] As the head pitches, rolls, and yaws, fluid in the canals sloshes around and triggers neural signals registering the motion. [. . .] Perhaps because we are terrestrial creatures, we use the gravity signal mostly to keep our bodies upright rather than to compensate for out-of-kilter visual input when they are not" (*How the Mind Works* [New York: Norton, 1997] 264).

Spinner

Pneumatic: "having to do with the spirit or soul" ("Pneumatic" [adj.], def. 3). See 1 Cor. 15.45: "Scripture [Gen. 2.7] says, 'The first man, Adam, became an animate being' [i.e., a living soul], whereas the last Adam [Jesus Christ, the all-inclusive Son of God] has become a life-giving spirit." *The Round Chaos; Spinner*

polestar or hound: a pair of storied binary stars—Polaris, "the point around which everything turns" and hence "a symbol of the self" (Jung, *Psychology and Alchemy* 188), and Sirius, or Sothis, the ambivalent *hound* associated with the tears of Isis and the annual, fructifying inundation of the Nile River (Jung, *Mysterium Coniunctionis* 20). *Servant of Nature*

polymorphous light: a mineralogical metaphor; radiant energy that crystallizes in two or more forms or systems, i.e., the divine as well as the human. *Hourglass*

the power of life: See Paul's description of Christ in Heb. 7.15-16: "the new priest who arises is one like Melchizedek, owing his priesthood not to a system of earthbound rules but to the power of a life that cannot be destroyed." *The Power of Life*

Precursor power vatic as a sling's: The speaker alludes to the biblical David, here not only the anointed, second king of Israel and Judah, but also—as an ancestor of Jesus—an oracle of all-consuming faith. See 1 Samuel 17.50: In his battle with the Philistine warrior, young "David proved the victor with his sling and stone; he struck Goliath down and gave him a mortal wound, though he had no sword." *Split-Minded*

Preferred the least action: In 1942, the American physicist Richard Feynman had found that "classical particles, like baseballs and billiard balls, [. . .] follow a least-action path through the universe. No matter how an object moved, it balanced out energies so as to use as little action as possible" (Fred Alan Wolf, *Taking the Quantum Leap* [New York: Harper, 1981] 196). *The Quantum Alice*

priest with his knife: Abraham, the father of Isaac, "who stretched out his hand and took the knife to kill his son [. . .]" (Gen. 22.11). *The Power of Life*

Primed as a tar: in colloquial parlance, "a sailor" ("Tar²" [n.], def.) prepared or made ready. *Spinner*

Primordial atoms that ravel smart: a reference not only to the 19th-century notion that *atoms* are nothing more than inner-directed, holistic spherules of force, but also to the current chip-based system of *smart* dust: "nanostructured flakes of porous silicon" that can self-assemble, mimic particles, and then spread into the atmosphere even as they collect and monitor computational data. See "Smart Dust," *UCSD Sailor Research Group* 13 Sept. 2009 <http://sailorgroup.ucsd.edu/research/smartdust>. *The Path of Least Action*

***Procyon* (pro-see-ahn)**: the little Dog Star. The Greek form combines *pro-*, before, and *kuon*, dog; hence, the star is called *Procyon* because it rises before Sirius. *Eros' Meal*

Psyche: not only the princess loved by Cupid, but also Mary in her role as Mother of God and as Sophia, the embodiment of both Wisdom and the afflicted soul. For a succinct overview of Mary's link to Sophia, see Baring and Cashford, *The Myth of the Goddess* 609-11. See also *Alchemical Studies* 335-37, where Jung explores the Gnostic interpretation of Psyche's relation to wholeness: "Expressed in the language of myth, Christ (the principle of masculine spirituality) perceives the sufferings of Sophia (i.e., the psyche) and thereby gives her form and existence. But he leaves her to herself so that she should feel the full force of her sufferings. What this means is that the masculine mind is content merely to perceive psychic suffering, but does not make itself conscious of the reasons behind it [. . .]." However, each participant in the agony of the Cross—Christ as well as Sophia—must become *aware* of the other's suffering, since "There can be no [reunified] consciousness without this act of discrimination [. . .]" (*Alchemical Studies* 336). *Astronaut*

puer (*poo*-ere): the *puer aeternus*, the divine boy who "can strike no roots in the world" because he "is, as it were, only a dream of the mother, an ideal which she soon takes back into herself, as we can see from the Near Eastern 'son-gods' like Tammuz, Attis, Adonis, and Christ" (Jung, *Symbols of Transformation* 258). *Orpheus' Rite*

Python of Apollo: In *The Bestiary of Christ,* having explained that Greece "had its mysterious and celestial serpents," and that "the nearest [snake] to the divine was that of Zagreus-Dionysus," while "the most infernal was the Python of Apollo" (154), Charbonneau-Lassay reminds us that "it is important not to forget the double aspect, good and evil, of the serpent" in the iconography of the Church (159). In fact, "Jesus advised his followers to be 'wise as serpents, and harmless as doves' [Matt. 10.16]. Here, once again, Christian symbolism goes hand in hand with older ideas which had made the serpent the ideograph of wisdom" (160). *The Set-Up*

pyx: "the container in which the consecrated wafer of the Eucharist is kept" ("Eucharist" [n.], def. 1a). *God's Semaphore*

quail that He bade, / Cobwebby hoarfrost, such dew as He laid: In the exodus from Egypt, the Lord bestowed upon the Israelites a catalogue of blessings. Thus, "That evening a flock of quails flew in and settled all over the camp, and in the morning a fall of dew lay all around it. When the dew was gone, there in the wilderness, fine flakes appeared, fine as hoar-frost on the ground" (Exod. 16.13-14)—in effect, the miraculous food that the people stored and ate "for forty years until they came to a land [Canaan] where they could settle [. . .]" (Exod. 16.35). *Eros' Meal*

quantum: in the *quantum* theory of matter, a pulse or packet that contains "a given [fixed] quantity of energy" (Davies, *Other Worlds* 32) and that functions as both "wave of probability" (64) and particle. *The Power of Life; The Quantum Alice*

quantum fluctuations: in the cosmic vacuum, tiny undulations that turned into the big bang. Malcolm W. Browne upholds this theory in "Physicists Confirm Power of Nothing, Measuring Force of Quantum Foam," *The New York Times* 21 Jan. 1997, New Eng. ed.: C6: "We are all quantum fluctuations. [. . .] That's the origin of us all and of everything in the universe, not just dark matter." *The Power of Life*

quark: any of a group of six subatomic particles, plus their anti-particles. Quarks are "heavy and strongly interacting, and make up nuclear matter" (Davies, *The Mind of God* 210). *Entwining the Light*

quaternal: a portmanteau word that blends the adjectives "quaternary" (four) and "eternal" (everlasting) and that, in this poem, identifies Christ as the quadripartite "unitary being who existed before man" and who represents "man's wholeness" (Jung, *Psychology and Alchemy* 162). *Tattoo*

Quill worm that tunnels: Cf. Jane Reynolds, Phil Gates, and Gaden Robinson, *365 Days of Nature and Discovery* (New York: Abrams, 1994) 55: "Quill worms build protective tubes of sand." *Orpheus' Rite*

quince: "a golden or greenish-yellow, hard, apple-shaped fruit of a small tree" ("Quince" [n.], def. 1)—here, the forbidden fruit of Gen. 2.16-17. *The Set-Up*

Ra (rah): in Egyptian mythology, "the sun god and principal deity" who is "usually depicted as having the head of a hawk and wearing the solar disk as a crown" ("Ra" [n.], def.). *Orpheus' Rite*

Rabid the Dog Star that yet shows the way: Here *the Dog Star* alludes not only to Sirius, "the brightest star in the sky" ("Sirius" [n.], def.), but also to the Christian parallel *Christus/canis*, since Christ is the watchdog of His flock. In addition, the term *Rabid* denotes the dog's "power to spread infection, especially rabies and diseases of the spleen." Thus, "Because of its rich symbolic context the dog is an apt [alchemical] symbol for the transforming substance" (Jung, *Mysterium Coniunctionis* 147n280). *Inmate of Space*

Raft snail that bubbles: The bubble raft snail *Janthina*, "too heavy to be supported by the surface tension [of the ocean] unaided, secretes a raft [or beam] of bubbles beneath which it hangs" (Cooke, *The Restless Kingdom* 71). *Orpheus' Rite*

rationed then His teat: Jesus shared His Eucharistic food like a mother. Thus, in *Jesus as Mother: Studies in the Spirituality of the Middle Ages* (1982; Berkeley: U of California P, 1984), Caroline Walker Bynum reports that "in medieval medical theory[,] breast milk is processed blood. [. . .] the loving mother, like the pelican who is also a symbol for Christ, feeds her child with her own blood" (132). *Trismegistus' Art*

razor shell that pries: a bivalve mollusc with an elongated shape like that of the straight *razor* from which the species takes its name. The *razor shell* uses its powerful foot to burrow beneath the sand. *Orpheus' Rite*

rebis (*ray*-bis): "The dual being born of the alchemical union of opposites" (masculine/feminine) and recognized "as a symbol of the self" (Jung, *Aion* 268). *Apostolates; Courtship; The Crowned Hermaphrodite; Gamonymous; God's Folly; Inmate of Space; Living in Curved Space; Tattoo; Trismegistus' Art*

Rebis that *shapely*: the spiritual hermaphrodite as an archetype of divine wholeness. *Inmate of Space*

***Reclaim God's archetype*:** The speaker would recover Christ as an authentic version of Eros, the Life Instinct. *God's Folly*

***Re-collects the torus*:** The *torus*, the universe conceived as a hyperdoughnut, is only one of the "strange topologies" that Michio Kaku predicates in *Hyperspace* 94-98 and that the speaker of this poem exploits to underscore the circular intricacies of the conglomerate self. Concerning the latter subject, in *Psychology and Western Religion*, Jung examines the crucial (psychological) phenomenon identified here, that of self-recollection. Thus, "the integration or humanization of the self is initiated from the conscious side," he asserts, "by our making ourselves aware of our selfish aims; we examine our motives and try to form as complete and objective a picture as possible of our nature. It is an act of self-recollection, a gathering together of what is scattered, of all the things in us that have never been properly related, and coming to terms with [ourselves] with a view to achieving full consciousness." Jung maintains that "we are forced to make this effort by the unconscious presence of the self, which is all the time urging us to overcome our unconsciousness" (159). *Living in Curved Space*

Red Damascene earth: in Cabalistic literature, the soil from which the first Adam was created (Jung, *Alchemical Studies* 318). *Damascene* is the adjectival form of Damascus, widely regarded as the oldest *continuously* inhabited city in the world. *Borderline Noun*

reeled out past her: Apparently the speaker became, like Christ, a "fisher of men" (Matt. 4.19) even as he crisscrossed Maya's web—"the illusory world of the senses"—beyond its deadly hub. See Jung, *Psychology and Alchemy* 217, fig. 108, and also 77, fig. 28, where Christ captures the Leviathan "with the sevenfold tackle of the line of David" and "with the crucifix as bait." *The Foliate Pebble*

regnant: As a symbol of Aphrodite's power, the myrtle is "prevalent" or "widespread" ("Regnant" [adj.], def. 3). *The Set-Up*

released Him to a plot / Akin to Golgotha; midmost the spot: In *Mysterium Coniunctionis*, Jung mentions that Jesus was buried at the navel or center of the Earth— in other words, on the hill of Golgotha (388). *God's Folly*

***Remnant of its coupling*:** The marriage of Ouranos (Father Heaven) and Gaea (Mother Earth) produced not only the human species (Hamilton, *Mythology* 64), but also the heavenly *Remnant* of End-time, the prophesied "hundred and forty-four thousand [. . .] ransomed as the firstfruits of humanity for God and the Lamb" (Rev.

14.3-5). *God's Folly*

> ***remnant that He skims*:** End-time's "ransomed" believer-priests, whom the Lamb, having come again to judge the living and the dead, shall "glide or pass swiftly and lightly over" ("Skim" [vt.], def. 4a). See Rev. 14.5: "No lie was found in their lips; they are faultless." *Crystal*

> **Resin of the wise *concealed in the drum*:** "a synonym for the transforming substance," the life force likened by the alchemists "to the 'glue of the world,'" a red gum [originally gum arabic] fixed as "the medium between mind and body and the union of both" (Jung, *Psychology and Alchemy* 161). Here, the *drum* is either Gaea's belly or Mary's womb. *The Foliate Pebble*

> ***resonant strings*:** See Brian Greene, *The Elegant Universe: Superstrings, Hidden Dimensions, and the Quest for the Ultimate Theory* (1999; New York: Vintage-Random, 2000) 143-44: "According to string theory, the properties of an elementary 'particle'—its mass and its various force charges—are determined by the precise resonant pattern of vibration that its internal string [i.e., its incredibly tiny, one-dimensional filament] executes." *Split-Minded*

> ***ribboned aster*:** Christ's latterday "astral" coheir—the "Citizen of the Cosmos"—modified by his intertwined strands of DNA. In *Alchemical Studies*, Jung asserts that, for Paracelsus, the Swiss physician and alchemist (1493-1541), "'The true man is the star [i.e., the heavenly light] in us'" (131). *The Foliate Pebble*

> **right side up:** a reference not only to the hierophant's bipedal stance and to the upright Eucharistic cup, but also to the eye's inverted retinal image. See *Catching the Light* 31-32, where Zajonc asks "How can the image on the retina be upside down when we see the world right side up?" and then theorizes that, at some point, "optics ends and the light of the body, that is the soul's activities, must be engaged in order for us to see the world right side up." *Liquid Metal Man*

> ***risen atoms smart*:** In *Taking the Quantum Leap*, throughout chapter 14, Wolf argues that atoms, being both conscious and curious, are also *smart*—i.e., "intelligent, alert, clever, [and] witty" ("Smart" [adj.], def. 4a). However, in this octet, the speaker's pun suggests that the *risen* or buoyant molecules of our being may also "cause sharp, stinging pain," or "be the source of such pain," since their transmutation—their *healing*—involves the Way of the Cross ("Smart" [vi.], def. 1a). *Trismegistus' Art*

> ***Rivers of water, belly that we plumb*:** in Gnostic symbolism, paradisal waters that pour into the world through the four gospels and that flow from "the belly of Christ" (Jung, *Aion* 215). Cf. John 7.37-38: "Jesus stood and cried aloud, 'If anyone is thirsty let him come to me; whoever believes in me, let him drink.'" *The Foliate Pebble*

> ***rook*:** In alchemical texts, the raven or *rook* symbolizes the *nigredo* or blackness—"the initial state" in the process of transformation, "either present from the beginning as a quality of the *prima materia*, the chaos or *massa confusa*, or else

produced by the separation (*solutio, separatio, divisio, putrefactio*) of the elements" (Jung, *Psychology and Alchemy* 230). *The Path of Least Action*

Root of itself: For the alchemists, the *prima materia* (the unknown substance) was—among its many symbolical names—"the One and the root of itself" (Jung, *Alchemical Studies* 139). See, for example, "Physica Trithemii" (*Theatrum chemicum*, vol. 1 [Strasbourg, 1659]) 391, where Gerhard Dorn declares that the One "is simple and consists of the number four" and, further, that this [the quaternity as designated unity] "is the centre of the natural wisdom, whose circumference, closed in itself, forms a circle: an immeasurable order reaching to infinity" (qtd. in Jung, *Alchemical Studies* 150-51). *The Foliate Pebble*

***root of its spawn*:** Cf. Jung, *Alchemical Studies* 195: "In psychological terms, [. . .] the self has its roots in the body, indeed in the body's chemical elements." *God's Folly*

***Rotund alembic, void that circumvents / Turbid residue*:** Like the circular form of the Hermetic vessel—i.e., the pelican, "in Christian iconography [. . .] a symbol of Christ" (Chevalier and Gheerbrant, *The Penguin Dictionary of Symbols* 746)—the self-organizing, complexified cosmos subjects its "distillate to sundry distillations so that the 'soul' or 'spirit' shall be extracted in its purest state" (Jung, *Psychology and Alchemy* 124). *The Cheshire of Sense*

***rotundum* (roh-*tun*-dum):** the "round, original form" of "the spiritual, inner and complete man" (C. G. Jung, *Mandala Symbolism*, trans. R. F. C. Hull [1959; Princeton: Princeton UP, 1973] 9-10). See also *Mysterium Coniunctionis* 140, where Jung remarks that "In alchemy Mercurius is the rotundum *par excellence*." *Entwining the Light*

the round chaos: In *Psychology and Alchemy*, Jung defines this idea as the primordial "life-mass," the "confused assortment of crude disordered matter" (144n59) that, containing all the elements, not only prefigures the gold, but also gives birth to the *lapis philosophorum*—the living philosophical stone (325). *The Round Chaos*

Rub away the pupil, beam not splinter: an ironic variation on Matt. 7.4-5: "how can you say to your brother, 'let me take the speck out of your eye,' when all the time there is that plank in your own? You hypocrite! First take the plank out of your own eye, and then you will see clearly to take the speck out of your brother's." Here, of course, the *pupil* refers not only to "the contractile circular opening, apparently black, in the center of the iris" ("Pupil[2]" [n.], def.), but also to the blemished "sprinter" of line 15, the Christian disciple himself. *Cinderdust*

Rubeous foetus: In the writings of the Cistercian monk Guillaume de Digulleville (1295-1358), "Gold, the royal colour, is attributed to God the Father; red to God the Son, because he shed his blood; and to the Holy Ghost green [. . .]" (Jung, *Psychology and Alchemy* 212-13). *Crystal*

Rumor of Rhea (*ree*-uh): the Phrygian Attis, the young dying son of the Great Mother, depicted by the Gnostics as a mystery god. Calling him "the dark rumor of

Rhea," the Gnostics further characterize him as the "'grain of mustard seed' that grows into the kingdom of God" and that is "present in the body." Jung explores the "magnitude" of this archetype in *Aion* 198-99. *Living in Curved Space*

***Rust of the metals*:** See Jung, *Psychology and Alchemy* 159: "In the alchemical view rust, like verdigris [its green, or greenish-blue, coating], is the metal's sickness. But at the same time this leprosy is [. . .] the basis for the preparation of the philosophical gold." Thus, "The paradoxical remark of Thales [c. 624-c. 546 BC] that the rust alone gives the coin its true value is a kind of alchemical quip, which at bottom only says that there is no light without shadow and no psychic wholeness without imperfection. To round itself out, life calls not for perfection but for completeness; and for this the 'thorn in the flesh' is needed, the suffering of defects without which there is no progress and no ascent." *Crystal*

***Saba* (*sah*-buh):** another name for the ancient kingdom of Sheba. Here, the word is used as a metonym for the Queen of Sheba, who visited King Solomon in order to experience his reputed wisdom. (See Kings 10.1-13.) *Servant of Nature*

***Sahel* (sah-*hel*):** a "region in NC Africa characterized by periodic drought" ("Sahel" [n.], def.). *Finite Infinite*

Salamander frolicking: In *Mysterium Coniunctionis*, Jung notes that the *salamander* is "the Mercurial serpent [. . .] whom the fire does not consume [. . .]" and who apparently signifies the alchemical process of calcination (441). However, in *The Bestiary of Christ*, Charbonneau-Lassay remarks that "Chastity and virginity also claim the salamander as emblem because they pass through the midst of the passions flaming around them without being burned" (177). In addition, the Middle Ages made this mythological, "lizard-like" reptile (175) "the image of Christ because of his kingship over fire" (179). For a vivid illustration of "a salamander frolicking in the fire," see Jung, *Psychology and Alchemy* 277, fig. 138. *Trismegistus' Art*

***Same syzygy forsworn that long we mourn*:** In the first stanza, the speaker momentarily grieves the loss of the forbidden *rebis*, i.e., the hermaphrodite—the self-contained, *unified* Adam/Eve *syzygy*, the divine "pair of [Edenic] opposites" ("Syzygy" [n.], def. 1). However, in the second stanza, he realizes implicitly that the Original Man, Adam, being both male and female, still remains "the bridge to knowledge of God," not only because he "consists of three parts": the rational, the psychic [the spiritual], and the earthly, but also because the all-inclusive Christ, "related to the Original Man," has already surpassed him as the exemplar of both unity *and* totality and hence as a symbol of the transcendent self (Jung, *Aion* 201). *Heir Presumptive*

***Sapientia in Her solar teak*:** The speaker imagines that the Queen of the South, "who came from the ends of the earth to hear the wisdom of Solomon" (Matt. 12.42), was conveyed by a sunship made of "hard, yellowish-brown wood [. . .]" ("Teak" [n.], defs. 1, 2). See also *Psychology and Alchemy* 378, where Jung notes—in a paraphrase of Vulgate, Cant. 6.9—that the Queen of the South, or *Sapientia*, "is said to have come from the east, like unto the morning rising." *The End of Ourselves*

Saturn's gramophone: the icy rings of the planet Saturn likened to the spiral grooves of a 78 rpm phonograph record, the latter figure of speech a synecdoche, but, here, a whole (the *gramophone*) used to signify a part (the disk or cylinder itself). *Saturn's Gramophone*

Savior of the twins: the Gnostic Jesus revealed "as a double personality, part of which rises up from the chaos or *hyle*, while the other part descends as pneuma [soul or vital spirit] from heaven" (Jung, *Aion* 79). *Jack-o'-Lantern*

scales that imbricate: The image evokes the thin, flat plates that overlap evenly on the outer protective covering of fishes. *Bio*

The scaly webwork of the creature's folds: the chitinous plates that cover the body of Ouroboros, "the dragon that devours, fertilizes, begets, slays, and brings itself to life again" (Jung, *Psychology and Alchemy* 372), the latter creature at once a self-described circle and, in the *opus alchymicum*, "a symbol uniting all opposites" (295). *In the Line of Melchizedek*

scarab: a unicorned sun-beetle. In *The Bestiary of Christ*, Charbonneau-Lassay describes the *scarab* as "the emblem of the swift, vivifying, and intelligent ray of the sun, the *spiritus et mens*, *logos* or *ratio* of the Ancients, that is, the breath of life, the soul, the understanding, the inspired word, reason" (335). *Borderline Noun; The Set-Up*

A scarab self-born: According to Jung, the *scarab*—"the black, winged dung beetle [. . .] held sacred by the ancient Egyptians" ("Scarab" [n.], def. 2a)—is "a creature born of itself" (*Psychology and Alchemy* 452). *An Image of an Image*

scintillae **(sin-till-ee)**: an alternate plural form of "scintilla"; in medieval alchemy, soul-sparks that reflect God's descent into matter. Jung describes this phenomenon in *Alchemical Studies*: According to the alchemists, "in the very darkness of nature a light is hidden, a little spark without which the darkness would not be darkness [. . .]. The light from above made the darkness still darker; but the *lumen naturae* [the divine spark buried in the darkness] is the light of darkness itself, which illuminates its own darkness, and this light the darkness comprehends [. . .]." In short, "Not separation of the natures [human as well as divine] but union of the natures was the goal of alchemy" (160-61). See also *Mysterium Coniunctionis* 491, where Jung identifies even further the conduit to such wholeness: "In the unconscious are hidden those 'sparks of light' (*scintillae*), the archetypes, from which a higher meaning can be 'extracted.' The 'magnet' that attracts the hidden thing is the self, or in this case the 'theoria' or the symbol representing it, which the adept uses as an instrument." *Elapid's Cowl*

Scroll like a boa: any of the seven Sapiential books of the Bible compared to an uncoiling serpent, the latter a universal ideogram of wisdom as well as a basic archetype "linked to the well-springs of life and the imagination" (Chevalier and

Gheerbrant, *The Penguin Dictionary of Symbols* 858). *The Quantum Alice*

Seahorse, ammonite, colubrid that braid: A spiraling pipefish, a coiled fossil shell, a spherical snake—all these phenomena either tend toward or exhibit a holistic circular pattern. *Eros' Meal*

Seahorse that shudders: The speaker highlights an often painful stage in the pregnancy of the male seahorse—after the female fish "lays her eggs in an armored chamber (marsupium)" of his belly, he "fertilizes the eggs"; broods them "for about four weeks, while they are nourished by secretions from the spongy wall of his brood pouch"; and then, "over a period of 24 hours, [. . .] undergoes a series of shuddering contractions," even as "the perfectly formed young seahorses are expelled in large numbers" (Reynolds, Gates, and Robinson, *365 Days of Nature and Discovery* 108). *Orpheus' Rite*

sealed Him in a grot: Cf. John 3.1, 19.38-42: After Jesus' death, Joseph of Arimathaea and Nicodemus "took the body of Jesus and wrapped it, with the spices [myrrh and aloes], in strips of linen cloth according to Jewish burial-customs. Now, at the place where he had been crucified there was a garden, and in the garden a new tomb, not yet used for burial. There, because the tomb was near at hand and it was the eve of the Jewish Sabbath, they laid Jesus." In *Jesus: The Evidence*, Wilson explains that "The nineteenth-century edicule [or 'little building'] within the [restored] Church of the Holy Sepulchre"—the latter edifice at one time located outside Jerusalem's walls—enshrines "what remains of the reputed tomb of Jesus" (140). *God's Folly*

Sealed His metallic sod: Although Christ has chosen "to grant, assign, or designate with a seal [or mark of authenticity]" His cinctured astronaut ("Seal[1]" [vt.], def. 6), Christ's glorified servant must still "join his suit halves" with a waist ring (Joels, Kennedy, and Larkin, *The Space Shuttle Operator's Manual* 3.11, 3.12). As Jung declares in *Symbols of Transformation* 236, "No man can change himself into anything from sheer reason; he can only change into what he potentially is." *Trismegistus' Art*

Secretes his liquid, deposits his fuzz, / Extrudes his trip lines as a trapdoor does: Declining, the sun emits its rays of light surreptitiously, even as the trapdoor spider issues its strands of silk. *Inmate of Space*

Secured the cosmos: Trismegistus' art: The speaker extols Hermes Trismegistus as first alchemist and emblematic magus. Grounded in the teachings of Christ, he himself has secured (i.e., "ensured," "acquired," or even "captured") holistic secrets of the cosmos through a similar alchemy—that of the visionary imagination ("Secure" [vt.], defs. 2, 4, 5). *Trismegistus' Art*

Selene's rebis: either Endymion, the androgynous shepherd-lover of the moon goddess Selene, or the Shuttle astronaut himself. *Tattoo*

The Self is a clock that never runs down: Cf. Jung, *Psychology and Alchemy*

120: "the life force that eternally renews itself" is like "the [cosmic] clock that never runs down." *Borderline Noun*

Self-sown: self-fertilized, i.e., spiritually renewed. *The Foliate Pebble*

Sepia threshold: fading, reddish-brown embers of the Big Bang. *The Cheshire of Sense*

The serpent has risen, as if on cue / Shall devour His tail: the resurrected Savior projected as the crowned Ouroboros, "the snake that bites its own tail," the latter image both a self-described circle and a symbol of totality (Jung, *Aion* 190). *Tabernacled*

Servant of Nature: See Jung, *Mysterium Coniunctionis* 49: "In the centre [of the earth] dwells the Archaeus, 'the servant of nature,'" who is hermaphroditic. Thus, Jung notes that, in the epilogue to the 'Novum lumen' of the alchemist Michael Sendivogius (1566-1636), "When you place a twelve-year-old boy side by side with a girl of the same age, and dressed the same, you cannot distinguish between them. But take their clothes off and the difference will become apparent." According to the latter example—which punctuates Sendivogius' theme and which Jung paraphrases here—"the centre consists in a conjunction of male and female." *Servant of Nature*

Set down His cup . . . there . . . and then left the room: an allusion to the Last Supper described in Luke 22.17-19 and to the "living water" extolled in John 4.10. See also Ralph Waldo Emerson's complaint in "Self-Reliance" that "now we are a mob. Man does not stand in awe of man, nor is the soul admonished to stay at home, to put itself in communication with the internal ocean, but it goes abroad to beg a cup of water of the urns of men" (*Emerson's Essays*, introd. Irwin Edman [1926; New York: Apollo-Crowell, 1961] 52). *A Cup of Water*

the set-up: God's eternal plan for humankind. *The Set-Up*

Shade encased in glass: Dressed in his Apollo spacesuit and wearing his plastic bubble helmet, the deployed astronaut seems a mere apparition as he moonwalks. *The Round Chaos*

shadow like the Goth: the inky darkness that pervades the cosmos, as well as the proclivity to evil that overclouds human nature. Jung illuminates the archetype of the *shadow* in *Aion*: "The shadow is a moral problem that challenges the whole ego-personality, for no one can become conscious of the shadow without considerable moral effort. To become conscious of it involves recognizing the dark aspects of the personality as present and real. This act is essential for any kind of self-knowledge [. . .]" (8). *Citizen of the Cosmos*

Shadow matter: clumps and halos of dark—i.e., invisible—*matter* that fills the universe. *The Cheshire of Sense*

the shafts of Eros (er-ahs): the arrows of desire, a symbol linked, in Greek mythology, with the god of love ("Eros" [n.], def.) and, in alchemy, with "the motif of wounding" and "sacrificial death" (Jung, *Mysterium Coniunctionis* 30-31). *Saturn's Gramophone*

shaman (shah-mun): either a priest or a magus or a holy man with supernatural powers. *Astronaut; Bio; Hourglass; Jack-o'-Lantern; The Round Chaos; Split-Minded; Trismegistus' Art*

She issues from Her nimbus Holy Writ: The speaker invokes the lunar nature not only of Gaea—since, according to the alchemists, "the earth [or Gaea] made the moon" (Jung, *Mysterium Coniunctionis* 130)—but also of the Blessed Virgin, who "is often compared with the Moon in Christian litanies and, in Christian iconography, is depicted as standing upon a crescent Moon" (Chevalier and Gheerbrant, *The Penguin Dictionary of Symbols* 243). *The Quantum Alice*

Shell like a nautilus; [. . .] / Crescent self-sown: Through circular—even serpentine—images, the speaker, a child of the sun as well as of the moon, identifies himself as both coheir of Christ and crowned hermaphrodite. The image of the Ouroboros ("the dragon who marries himself") as a symbol of self-origination and that of the healing serpent of Moses as a precursor of the crucified Christ also figure here. See Jung, *Mysterium Coniunctionis* 293n138. *The Foliate Pebble*

Sheol (she-ohl): In *Handbook to the Gospels*, John Wijngaards helpfully discriminates between the hell of the eternally damned and *Sheol*, "'the place of the dead,' the home (in Jewish theology) of all the dead [. . .]. When we say that Jesus descended into hell we mean only (in the terminology of the Bible) that he was truly dead; he was no longer in the 'land of the living' but went down into the 'land of the dead'" (244-45), as every sojourner must. *The Foliate Pebble; Living in Curved Space*

She sculpts an organ suited to its gene: Cf. Zajonc, *Catching the Light* 341: "Light, ever active, created the eye. It sculpted an organ suited to itself, like the streaming water shaping the stones over and through which it flows. Had light not 'seen' man, we should never have seen the light." *Saturn's Gramophone*

She washed His feet until her soul was clean: See John 12.1-3: "Six days before the Passover festival Jesus came to Bethany, where Lazarus lived whom he had raised from the dead. There a supper was given in his honour, at which Martha served, and Lazarus sat among the guests with Jesus. Then Mary [the sister of Martha] brought a pound of very costly perfume, pure oil of nard, and anointed the feet of Jesus and wiped them with her hair, till the house was filled with the fragrance." *An Image of an Image*

shift my mass: Nick Strobel clarifies this subject in Chapter 5, titled "Mass and Weight," on his Web site *Astronomy Notes*: Although the terms *weight* and *mass* are used interchangeably in common discourse, in scientific terminology there is a "distinct difference" between the two concepts. "The *weight* of an object [equals the] force of gravity felt by that object," whereas "the *mass* of an object is the amount of matter [that] the [selfsame] object has." Thus, if an astronaut weighs himself, at first "on the Earth's surface and then on the Moon's surface," his *weight* on the Moon "will be about six times less than [it will be] on the earth"; however, since "the number of atoms in his body has not changed," his *mass* will remain "the same at the two places" (11 May 2001, 10 July 2015 <http://www.astronomynotes.com/gravappl/s4.htm>). *Astronaut*

ships' wakes in the bay: The NASA astronaut Joseph P. Allen supplies his own context for this image in "Joe's Odyssey," *Omni* (June 1983) 63: "You see layers as you look down. You see clouds towering up. You see their shadows on the sunlit plains, and you see a ship's wake in the Indian Ocean and brush fires in Africa and a lightning storm walking its way across Australia. You see the reds and the pinks of the Australian desert, and it's just like a stereoscopic view of all nature, except you're a hundred ninety miles up" (qtd. in Kelley, ed., *The Home Planet* 59). *Inmate of Space*

Shroud like a hood, as hierodules decree: "Inanna, or Ishtar as she was called in northern Sumeria, was one of the three great goddesses of the Bronze Age, the others being Isis of Egypt and Cybele of Anatolia. [. . .] Inanna relates the Neolithic Great Mother to the Biblical Eve, [to] Sophia [the Hebrew Hokhmah, or Wisdom], and [to] Mary." Among Inanna's many titles were "Queen of Heaven and Earth" and "Hierodule [i.e., temple slave] of Heaven" (Baring and Cashford, *The Myth of the Goddess* 176). *Eros' Meal*

shuttlewalk His beat: Shuttle astronauts patrol Jesus' *beat*, their assigned route in low-Earth orbit. The transitive verb, a neologism, suggests a cheerful form of (cosmic) police authority, as in the English-language idiom "walk his beat." *Tattoo*

side lanced like a cyst: In John 19.34-37, after the death of Jesus, "one of the soldiers stabbed his side with a lance, and at once there was a flow of blood and water. [. . .] this happened in fulfillment of the text in Scripture: [. . .] 'They shall look on him whom they pierced.'" *The Power of Life*

sight's Pandora: In Greek mythology, *Pandora*, the first mortal woman, opened a box and inadvertently let all human ills escape. Thus, *sight's Pandora* is the purveyor of tainted perception that gropes in the dark. *Entwining the Light*

Sigil like the solstice: "a seal" or an image—here, the stamped figure of the Summer solstice—"supposedly having some mysterious power in magic or astrology" ("Sigil" [n.], defs. 1, 2). See also Chevalier and Gheerbrant, *The Penguin Dictionary of Symbols* 892: "The Summer solstice (around 21 June) marks the apogee of the Sun's transit when it is at its zenith and stands at its highest in the sky." In Christian iconography, "This was the day chosen to celebrate the festival of the Sun." Understandably, then, "To the degree to which Christ [the Lord of Time] is compared with the Sun, he is depicted as the Summer solstice." *Spinner*

Simon's canopy: See Matt. 17.1-7: "Jesus took [*Simon*] Peter, James, and John the brother of James, and led them up a high mountain where they were alone; and in their presence he was transfigured; his face shone like the sun, and his clothes became white as the light. And they saw Moses and Elijah appear, conversing with him. Then Peter spoke: 'Lord,' he said, 'how good it is that we are here! If you wish it, I will make three shelters [tabernacles] here, one for you, one for Moses, and one for Elijah.'" Of course, as Luke 9.33 indicates, Peter, though well-intentioned, "spoke without knowing what he was saying," since he mistakenly regarded both Moses and Elijah as equal in stature to Jesus. *Hourglass*

simple: either a medicinal herb or the medicine obtained from such a plant. *A Cup of Water*

Since life and death like spouses intertwine, / [. . .] Or climb down space or pray the unit stay: The entire stanza develops an analogy—a sort of riddled metaphysical conceit—that links the act of dying on the Cross with birth, transubstantiation, space flight, and sexual consummation. See Nilsson and Lindberg, *Behold Man* 53-55 and Kerrod, *Space Walks* 18-23. *A Cloud in Slow Motion*

singularity: in astrophysics, the point of infinite compression at which space and time cease to exist. *Galactic Pilgrim; Trismegistus' Art*

sintered: here, reduced to slag, dross, or cinders. *The Quantum Alice*

Sirius: Also called the Dog Star and Sothis (*so*-this), *Sirius* is the brightest star seen from Earth. In the ancient Egyptian story of Isis (*eye*-sis) and Osiris (oh-*sigh*-ris)—a "lunar mystery"—the rising of the Dog Star (i.e., of Isis manifest as the star Sothis) "brought Osiris back to life" (Baring and Cashford, *The Myth of the Goddess* 233-34). *The End of Ourselves; Eros' Meal*

Skein of the Shekinah: *Skein*, "a quantity of thread or yarn wound in a coil" ("Skein" [n.], def. 1a), connotes, in this context, both the helical pattern of the hereditary molecule (DNA) and—as modified by the prepositional phrase—the descent of humankind from "the manifestation of the presence of God" ("Shekinah" [n.], def.). See Baring and Cashford, *Myth of the Goddess* 640: "The Shekhinah [an alternate spelling] was identified by the Kabbalists with the radiance of the Holy Spirit [. . .]. The Shekhinah is immanent in the human soul as its divine 'ground' or radiant 'body', and can be revealed personally to men and women. She is their deepest self, the holy presence of 'the glory of God' within them. The sacred marriage in Kabbalism is [. . .] the union of the soul with this Holy Spirit. Through the radiant light of the Shekhinah everything is linked to everything else, as if connected through a luminous skein of being." (Here, the word is pronounced "Shuh-*keye*-na.") *Inmate of Space*

slipknot like a sling: "a knot made so that it will slip along the rope [. . .] around which it is tied" ("Slipknot" [n.], def.)—in other words, along a rope with a loop not unlike that of a *sling*. Here, of course, the more or less circular figure of the loop not only evokes young King David's storied *sling* (1 Sam. 17.50), but also becomes the speaker's psychological projection of the Christian Savior, since "the circle is a well-known symbol for God" (Jung, *Aion* 195). *Heterotic*

Slipper Limpets settle: The speaker pays tribute to molluscs that colonize as they will. See S. Peter Dance, *The World's Shells: A Guide for Collectors* (New York: McGraw-Hill, 1976) 82-83: "Some gastropods have the experience of being progressively male, hermaphrodite and female. The best known example of this presumably delightful sexual condition is *Crepidula fornicata* Linnaeus, the Slipper Limpet. It is not unusual to find chains of specimens of this pest of oyster beds in which the topmost and youngest specimen is a male, the next a young female, the middle ones [sequential] hermaphrodites[,] and the lowest ones female." *Heterotic*

Snowy quintessence: the purified spirit embodied by the suited astronaut, who, like the mercurial life-force, "flies like solid white snow." See *Alchemical Studies* 214. *Astronaut*

***solar calèche* (kuh-*lesh*)**: a metonym for Christ as sun-god. A *calèche* or calash is "a light, low-wheeled carriage, usually with a folding top" ("Calash" [n.], def. 1). *Inmate of Space*

Sol's sea goat worn: the constellation Capricorn, "which is depicted as a goat with the tail of a fish" and "has the form of a large faint triangle considered by the ancients to be the Gate of Heaven" (Engelbrektson, *Stars, Planets, and Galaxies* 36). *Heir Presumptive*

Some Cheshire in the sky, its whiskers shorn: the *Cheshire* cat from Lewis Carroll's *Alice's Adventures in Wonderland*, here transmogrified into a black hole. According to the physicist John Archibald Wheeler (1911-2008), "black holes have no hair" because they possess "only mass, angular momentum, and electric charge" and display "no trace of what they [have] consumed." See David M. Harland, *The Big Bang: A View from the 21st Century* (Chichester: Springer-Praxis, 2003) 228. *Heir Presumptive*

Some doors open from the inside, *Castor*: a final clause—the speaker's self-directed apostrophe—that superimposes images of copulation, birth, and affectivity. Cf. Thomas Bezansen, "Endpoint," *IONS Noetic Sciences Review* 2 (1999): 64: "Some doors open only from the inside." In this poem, the crucial addition is *Castor* (the twin brother of Pollux), a hyphenated Everyman belonging both to Heaven and to Earth. *The Foliate Pebble*

Some heron's stone that at the threshold pings: a pithy variation on a familiar totem: the Great Blue Heron as a manifestation of the world-transforming Spirit, here not only the possessor, but also the deliverer, of alchemy's "animate [or magnetic] stone," a gift that "means nothing less" than the speaker/dreamer's connubial "vow to the self" (Jung, *Psychology and Alchemy* 186). For an alternate interpretation, see Charbonneau-Lassay, *The Bestiary of Christ* 270-71: "The heron's preference for solitary places has [...] made of it one of Christian symbolism's rare living examples of silence, a silence which is precious because it leads the human being from reflection to wisdom. Medieval artists, especially the heraldists, represented this idea by showing the heron standing and holding in its beak a stone that keeps it from uttering a sound. This stone was called by the Ancients *leucochryse* (white crystal), a gem of a pale golden color, traversed by white lines, which was believed to help the person who carried it to acquire wisdom." In both readings, the metallic *ping* evokes the sonic key to higher consciousness. *Split-Minded*

some hollow bottle: a trickster's container "having an empty space, or only air, within it" and "depressed below the surrounding surface" ("Hollow" [adj.], defs. 1, 2). In this stanza, the innominate Shuttle astronaut has not yet perceived that "The work of the [indwelling] Spirit is to build up a habitation for God" (Murray, *The Spirit of Christ* 235-36). *The Power of Life*

Some hood upon a tree: either Christ's tunic—a "seamless" garment (John 19.24)—or Mary's cloak. The speaker also exploits a pun: the slang shorthand for "hoodlum" ("Hood²" [n.], def.). *Spacetime's Handkerchief*

Some Johannine image: See, for instance, 1 John 3.2: "Here and now, dear friends, we are God's children; what we shall be has not yet been disclosed, but we know that when it is disclosed we shall be like him, because we shall see him as he is." *The Round Chaos*

Some Maya that spins to Polestar or soul: The "eternal weaver of the sensory world of the senses" connects Earth to Polaris (the North Star) and matter to *soul* or spirit. See Jung, *Psychology and Alchemy*, fig. 108. Like the archetypal tree itself, wholeness entails "growth from below upwards and from above downwards" (Jung, *Alchemical Studies* 272). *Liquid Metal Man*

Some sapphirine premise: the heaven-sent conviction that "The [eternal] Word is Spirit-breathed" (Murray, *The Spirit of Christ* 228). Murray explains that "In the creation of the world, it was the work of the Spirit to put Himself into contact with the dark and lifeless matter of chaos, and by His quickening energy to give it the power of life and fruitfulness. It was only after it had been vitalized by Him that the Word of God gave it form and called forth all the different types of life and beauty we now see. In the creation of man, it was also the Spirit that was breathed into the body that had been formed from the ground. The Spirit united itself with what would otherwise be dead matter" (166). *Courtship*

Some simple truth conglomerate as pi: an ironic utterance. In Mathematics, *pi* is an irrational number, the "decimal expansion" of which "is unending and [only] seemingly random" (Davies, *The Mind of God* 104). *The Quantum Alice*

some transcendental clock: "a species of clock whose hands move unceasingly, [. . .] a *perpetuum mobile*"—in effect, a cosmic *clock* (Jung, *Psychology and Alchemy* 104-05). *Bowknot*

Son of the Son: the individual percipient reborn through Christ. In other words, like a father, the Savior teaches the speaker how to be a son. Cf. Eph. 1.5: "He [Yahweh] destined us to be His adopted sons through Jesus Christ." *Tattoo*

soror (*soar*-or): the Latin word for "sister"—here, specifically, the *soror mystica*, the adept who, along with the alchemist, seeks the holistic conjunction of opposites. See *Psychology and Alchemy* 280, fig. 140. *Bio*

spa: "any place, esp. a health resort, having a mineral spring" ("Spa" [n.], def.). *Orpheus' Rite*

Spacetime's handkerchief: Saint Veronica's napkin, as well as a magician's substitute cape. *Spacetime's Handkerchief*

Spacetime's Leviathan: in the Bible, "a sea monster," either reptile or whale ("Leviathan" [n.], def. 1). In alchemy, *Leviathan* becomes, like the raven, a symbol of the transforming substance. See Jung, *Psychology and Alchemy* 134, 464. *The Path of Least Action*

The spagyric foetus: The word *spagyric* refers to an alchemical process that both separates and combines (Jung, *Mysterium Coniunctionis* 481n91). Thus, the *spagyric foetus* ascends into Heaven that it may become a spirit from a body and then descends to earth that it may become a body again. Cf. John 3.13: "'No one ever went up into heaven except the one who came down from heaven, the Son of Man whose home is in heaven.'" *Courtship*

Sphere of the Trinity: The Neo-Pythagoreans held that God, as the world-soul, "is a circle or sphere." The round nature of the stone suggests the lunar or feminine aspect of God (Jung, *Psychology and Alchemy* 325). *The Foliate Pebble*

split-minded in the pan: See Harth, *Windows on the Mind* 186: "in the relatively featureless structure of the cerebral cortex, the division between left and right *hemispheres* is the most salient aspect of the [human] brain's anatomy." Thus, "the left brain half turns out to dominate most of our decision making and our linguistic transactions" (189), while the right hemisphere [in the brain*pan* or cranium] specializes in "functions that all have to do in one way or another with manipulative skills" (190). *Split-Minded*

spool in the sand / Ringed with salmon pink: The *spool* or wheel is a symbol of the totalistic Uroboros, "the snake that bites its own tail" (Jung, *Aion* 190). In these lines, the syntactically ambiguous participial phrase describes the python, the pelican, and the *sand*. In effect, the speaker fuses the image of the pelican that Charbonneau-Lassay delineates in *The Bestiary of Christ* 258 and the photograph of the *salmon pink* Avicenna viper (camouflaged beneath matching desert *sand*) that Bauchot features in *Snakes* 83. *The Set-Up*

spring-point of Pisces, goat or teddy: In *Aion*, Jung suggests that, "to the extent that Christ was regarded as the new aeon, it would be clear to anyone acquainted with astrology that he was born as the first fish of the Pisces era, and was doomed to die as the last ram [or (scape)goat] [...] of the declining Aries era. [Thus,] Matt. 27.15ff. hands down this mythologem in the form of the old sacrifice of the seasonal god" (90).

Concerning the shifting *spring-point*, Jung calculates that "Astrologically the beginning of the next aeon [. . .] falls between A.D. 2000 and 2200" (94n84). The *teddy* mentioned here is Ursa Minor, or the Lesser Bear, the latter constellation being the home of Polaris, the North Star, as well as the storied co-ruler (with Aquarius) of the approaching age. *Citizen of the Cosmos*

the sprinter: God's athlete, as in Heb. 12.1-2: "And what of ourselves? With all these witnesses to faith around us like a cloud, we must throw off every encumbrance, every sin to which we cling, and run with resolution the race for which we are entered, our eyes fixed on Jesus, on whom faith depends from start to finish [. . .]." *Cinderdust*

Sprung from out Her Tree like a statue sawn: In *Symbols of Transformation*, Jung demonstrates that a "common mother-symbol is the wood of life [. . .], or tree of life. The tree of life may have been, in the first instance, a fruit-bearing genealogical tree, and hence a kind of tribal mother. Numerous myths say that human beings came from trees, and many of them tell how the hero was enclosed in the maternal tree-trunk, like the dead Osiris in the cedar-tree, Adonis in the myrtle, etc." (219). The speaker also alludes to the mandrake, a southern European plant "formerly thought to have magical powers because of its fancied resemblance to the human body" ("Mandrake" [n.], def. 2). See, for example, John Donne's *Song*— first published in 1633—in *Donne: Poetical Works*, ed. Sir Herbert Grierson (1933; London: Oxford UP, 1967) 8: "Goe, and catch a falling starre, / Get with child a mandrake roote" (ll. 1-2). *God's Folly*

Stag and unicorn in the forest meet: symbols of soul, spirit, and body, respectively (Jung, *Mysterium Coniunctionis* 5). For a vivid illustration of this alchemical equation, see Jung, *Psychology and Alchemy* 436, fig. 240. *Astronaut*

the static in the horn: the cosmic fireball radiation that Arno Penzias and Robert Wilson detected in 1965 with a large horn antenna "built like an oversized ear trumpet" and "sensitive to faint radio whispers that travel through the universe" (Jastrow, *God and the Astronomers* 20). *The Cheshire of Sense*

stiffed: a curtailed form that conflates the intransitive verb "stiffen" (to make or become rigid) and the idiomatic noun "stiff" (corpse). *A Cloud in Slow Motion*

Still an image of an image of God: See *Aion* 37-38, where Jung notes that "The *imago Dei* imprinted on the soul, not on the body, is [but a trace or vestige,] an image of an image, [as Origen (185-254) reasons,] 'for my soul is not directly the image of God, but is made after the likeness of the former image.' Christ, on the other hand, is the true image of God, after whose likeness our inner man [i.e., the God-image, or *Spirit* of God, that indwells the mind] is made, invisible, incorporeal, incorrupt, and immortal." Here, Jung both quotes and paraphrases excerpts from four of Origen's works: *Contra Celsum*, *In Lucam homiliae*, *De principiis*, and *In Genesim homiliae*. *An Image of an Image*

Still galaxies slide or mix in the light, [. . .] / Courtship in the cosmos the strangest rite: Cf. Begley, "When Galaxies Collide" 5: "Galaxies close enough together to feel each other's gravity undergo a coy, slow courtship. When they meet, they might slide by, passing in the night like cosmic strangers. But they might, instead, collide. Our own Milky Way is now swallowing a dwarf galaxy called Sagittarius." *Courtship*

Still the trumpeter orchestrates His blare: In Rev. 11.15-19, after six angels had sounded their trumpets in order to signal apocalyptic events, the seventh angel "blew his trumpet; and voices were heard in heaven shouting: 'The sovereignty of the world has passed to our Lord and his Christ, and he shall reign for ever and ever!'" *Galactic Pilgrim*

Stochastic: "of, pertaining to, or arising from chance; involving probability; random" ("Stochastic" [adj.], def. 1). *A Cloud in Slow Motion; The Round Chaos*

a stone at its core: in alchemy, the philosophers' *stone* taken as a symbol of the unified self, i.e., "of the inner Christ, of God in man" (Jung, *Alchemical Studies* 96). *A Cloud in Slow Motion*

stone in the seal: "a wax wafer [. . .] bearing the impression of some official design" ("Seal" [n.], def. 1)—here, that of the mysterious *lapis*, "the stone that is no stone" (*Alchemical Studies* 291n9), an Hermetic symbol "correlated with Christ" (292). See also 1 Peter 2.5: "Come, and let yourselves be built, as living stones, into a spiritual temple; become a holy priesthood, to offer spiritual sacrifices acceptable to God through Jesus Christ." *Spinner*

The stone that has a spirit: the Hermetic *lapis*, "the figure [of Christ] veiled in matter" (Jung, *Alchemical Studies* 247). *A Cup of Water; Split-Minded*

stone that heated dries: a reference to "the motif of torture"—a crucial element in "the phenomenology of the individuation process as the alchemists experienced it" and to one "gruesome" recipe in particular: "the drying of a man over a heated stone" (Jung, *Alchemical Studies* 328-29). Jung notes that, ironically, it is the artifex himself who, having projected himself into the material substance—the "stone"—of the opus, "cannot endure the torments" (329). *Orpheus' Rite*

The story of light has yet to be told: See *Catching the Light* 36-37, where Zajonc paraphrases Matt. 6.22-23: "Our light, a light of meaning, fashions a world, forms it from the light of day. If our light be darkness—be evil—then we bring darkness and evil into our whole body, personal and social. If it be light—be good—then health flows into us, and into the world." *Eros' Meal*

strand that Ge enshrines: either the speaker, the human species, or Earth itself, each but a single string—a twisted thread—in the cosmic coil. *Living in Curved Space*

Strange luminescences, traces of day: Cf. Kelley, ed., *The Home Planet* 61, where the Soyuz cosmonaut Valeri V. Ryumin, while "[f]lying above the planet," observes not only "the strange, flickering luminescence before sunrise near the equator"—a phenomenon that "resembles the northern lights"—but also "the brown shadows on the day side of the Earth that are constantly changing." *Inmate of Space*

Striated the belly: i.e., the postpartum stomach, its skin either stretch-marked or wrinkled. *Tattoo*

Stricken integer: what the mind had spanned: Beset by the "Plosive cumuli" of line 13—here, a synchronistic phenomenon, i.e., the "meaningful coincidence" of a psychic and a physical state (Jung, *Synchronicity* 100); in effect, a *"cross-connection"* without a cause (11)—the speaker had somehow channeled the fourth factor in a disturbed quaternity. See also Jung, *Psychology and Alchemy* 161-62: "The one joins the three [body, soul, and spirit] as the fourth [the androgynous original man or Anthropos of Gnostic philosophy] and thus produces the synthesis of the four in a unity [. . .]." *Hourglass*

strigil (strij-ill): "an instrument of bone, metal, etc. used by the ancient Greeks and Romans for scraping the skin during a bath" ("Strigil" [n.], def.). *Heterotic*

string(s): In *The Whole Shebang: A State-of-the-Universe(s) Report* (New York: Simon, 1997), Timothy Ferris indicates that, according to superstring theories, "subatomic particles are actually tiny strings made of space. [. . .] Strings are so small that when viewed from a distance—meaning at any wavelength of light or any other form of electromagnetic illumination—they 'look like' infinitesimal particles" (220). *Living in Curved Space; Split-Minded*

Styx: in Greek mythology, "the [icy-cold] river encircling Hades over which Charon ferries the souls of the dead" ("Styx" [n.], def.). *Navel*

Sublunary vessel: Mary and the speaker alike are presented as "terrestrial" or "earthly" offspring of the moon ("Sublunary" [adj.], defs. 1, 2). Each is also construed as being "the receiver or repository of some [divine] spirit or influence" ("Vessel" [n.], def. 2). Concerning Christ's imprint upon the coheirs of His heavenly kingdom, see Murray, *The Spirit of Christ* 83-85: "In virtue of His having perfected in Himself a new holy human nature on our behalf, He [Christ] could now communicate what previously had no existence—a life at once human and divine." In other words, "We have received the Spirit of Jesus to stream into us, to stream through us, and to stream forth from us in rivers of blessing." *The Power of Life*

Submersed in its membrane: i.e., in the cell membrane. Inside it is the protoplasm, "a semifluid, viscous, translucent colloid" ("Protoplasm" [n.], def.), the essential substance of all cells now differentiated into the cytoplasm and the nucleoplasm. See also *Behold Man* 10, where Nilsson and Lindberg observe that "A cell can be thought of as an independent individual belonging to the larger organization which the body represents. It is a being with a life of its own [. . .]." *Tabernacled*

substance that gray, / Stray infinity, he must stand away: Overwhelmed by "Some Johannine image" not unlike the celestial vision recounted in John 20.19—"Jesus came and stood among them"—the speaker must momentarily sidestep its presence, the latter apparition being but a random or an "isolated" occurrence ("Stray" [adj.], def. 2). *The Round Chaos*

substantiated, slain: the essence of Christ, and also of either Sophia or Mary the Mother of God, embodied and verified, paradoxically, through their suffering and (psychological) death. *Living in Curved Space*

such a tint / As salves my eye: The light produces in the Christian athlete a collyrium, an eyewash that enables the "anointed" adept "to see the secrets better" (Jung, *Alchemical Studies* 75-76). *Liquid Metal Man*

Such bread as He had wed: the precursor Eucharist—the Living Bread—reified at the Last Supper. *Citizen of the Cosmos*

Such noise inside the horn: an allusion to the cosmic fireball radiation that Arno Penzias and Robert Wilson had detected in 1965. The discovery was made with a large horn antenna "built like an oversized ear trumpet" and "sensitive to faint radio whispers that travel through the Universe" (Jastrow, *God and the Astronomers* 20). *Tabernacled*

Sundered from all secondness: Meister Eckhart (1260?-1327?) defines the mystic seeker's exemplary union with God in *Works*, trans. C. de B. Evans, vol. 1 (London, 1924) 247-48: "'Love him as he is: a not-spirit, a not-person, a not-image; as a sheer, pure, clear One, which he is, sundered from all secondness; and in this One let us sink eternally, from nothing to nothing. So help us God. Amen'" (qtd. in Jung, *Aion* 193). *Cinderdust*

swing or steady: two theories that posit the origin of the universe and that Davies explains in *The Mind of God*: oscillating, in which "the universe varies as it expands and contracts in a cyclic manner" (52), and *steady*-state, in which the universe has neither beginning nor end because "the average density of matter [. . .] remains unchanged"—in other words, the law of conservation of energy is (supposedly) not violated since "the positive energy of the created matter" is "compensated exactly by the enhanced negative energy of the creation field" (55-56). Davies shows why scientists have rejected both views in favor of an inflationary model in which "a little bubble of space-time [. . .] 'inflated' at a fantastic rate to produce a big bang" (70). See also Ferris, *The Whole Shebang* 229-44. *Citizen of the Cosmos*

Synonymous His bride: Christ and His tabernacled coheirs revealed as One Body. *Citizen of the Cosmos*

***syzygy* (*siz-*uh-jee):** paired opposites that represent wholeness—e.g., Mars and Venus. *Heir Presumptive*

Tabernacled now: Christ indwells His believer-priest. As Murray reminds us in *The Spirit of Christ*: "Each of us must learn to know that there is a Holiest of All in that temple which we are" (210). *A Cloud in Slow Motion*

tattoo "I in You"/ Wheel like a heart: a cardioid (a wheel shaped *like a heart* with a rounded tip) ingrained upon the flesh of the speaker and enfolding, inside its disk, a promise of everlasting spiritual love. Cf. John 14.18-20: "'In a little while the world will see me no longer, but you will see me; because I live, you too will live; then you will know that I am in my Father, and you in me and I in you.'" *Tattoo*

tee: the mound or hill, shaped like the four-square letter "T," where Christ was crucified and Adam buried; in other words, a Christian paraphrase of an ancient Greek concept—the omphalos, the "rounded stone in Apollo's temple at Delphi, regarded as the center [i.e., the navel] of the world" ("Omphalos" [n.], def.). *The Crowned Hermaphrodite*

teleosts (*tee*-lee-*ahsts*): groups of fishes with bony skeletons. *Bio*

Teleport Ge's retort: Teleportation is "the theoretical transportation of matter through space by converting it into energy and then reconverting it at the terminal point" ("Teleportation" [n.], def.). In *Space-Time and Beyond*, Bob Toben, "in conversation" with the physicists Jack Sarfatti and Fred Wolf, explains that, since "Every action in 'real' time is an indefinite sequence of materializations and dematerializations on the microscopic quantum level," and since the latter phenomena "occur faster than the speed of light and in such great numbers that perception of this action is continual," it is not inconceivable that "Teleportation could result from a giant quantum jump" (80). However, in "Living in Curved Space," the speaker, commuting "from one space-time path to another," achieves this feat even as the hyphenated Castor did—through the imagination of faith no less than through the "coherence" of "all the constituent particles" (*Space-Time and Beyond* 156). Here, of course, the earth goddess *Ge's retort* refers not only to the speaker's self-reflexive human response to Yahweh's "celestial utterance," but also to the astronaut's goal-oriented function as *Ge's* transformative alchemical *vas*. (Incidentally, in this poem, the name of the goddess is pronounced *gee*.) *Living in Curved Space*

Tellus: the Roman goddess of the earth identified with the Greek Gaea. *Finite Infinite*

Temenos (*teh*-meh-*nahs*): in Greek mythology, a sacred place; "a taboo area" where one can "meet the unconscious"—here, the womb of the mother (Jung, *Psychology and Alchemy* 54). *The Crowned Hermaphrodite*

tertiary key: the speaker himself viewed as an offspring of Christ, the second Adam. *Bio*

tesseract: an unraveled four-dimensional hypercube arranged as a three-dimensional cross, as in Salvador Dali's 1954 oil-on-canvas painting *Crucifixion (Corpus Hypercubus)*, where the artist depicts Christ "as being crucified on a tesseract." See Kaku, *Hyperspace* 72, fig. 3.7. *Crystal*

Tethered the unit—minuscule (mi-*nus*-kyool), immense— / That on the

***chaos stands*:** a paraphrase as well as a conflation of two indelible images—of the NASA astronaut Edward White, floating in low-Earth orbit above the Indian Ocean, in 1965 (Kerrod, *Space Walks* 18), and of Mercurius, alchemy's world-creating spirit, as "the [rejuvenated] sun-moon hermaphrodite (*rebis*), standing on the (round) chaos" (Jung, *Psychology and Alchemy* 244, fig. 125). *The Cheshire of Sense*

that man at Uz: Cf. Job 1.1: "There lived in the land of Uz a man of blameless and upright life named Job, who feared God and set his face against wrongdoing." *Inmate of Space*

That we may rise in loving bondage free: See Jung, *Alchemical Studies* 52: For Saint Paul and the nihilistic 19th-century philosopher Friedrich Nietzsche alike, the consciousness of being invisibly centered "delivers one from the bondage of the blood." *The Crowned Hermaphrodite*

Their androgyne: Christ, "the man encompassed by a woman" (Jung, *Mysterium Coniunctionis* 125)—in his divine androgyny, the eternal repetition of "the true hermaphroditic Adam" (16). *Tattoo*

Their essence—tabernacled: coil or rod—: a veiled reference to Christian discipleship and the Baptism of the Spirit. Thus, in honeybee silk glands, proteins are ordered into "a well-defined coiled coil molecular structure"; by contrast, in bumblebee silk glands, "the majority of the proteins are arranged into birefringent [i.e., light-splitting] fibrous rods" (Tara D. Sutherland, Sarah Weisman, Andrew A. Walker, and Stephen T. Mudie, "The Coiled Coil Silk of Bees, Ants, and Hornets," *Wiley Online Library* 9 Aug. 2011: 446-47, Wiley Periodicals, Inc., 2 Sept. 2014 <http://www.academia.edu/1491441>). In addition, both *coil* and *rod* function here as mammalian gender symbols: the feminine ring and the masculine pole. Apparently the speaker, a believer-priest, regards the human body as "God's temple" (1 Cor. 3.16), where "the Spirit of the God-man, Jesus Christ"—the *essence* of His reasoning mammals—now dwells (Murray, *The Spirit of Christ* 84). *An Image of an Image*

Then a high deep blue that He mixed with green: In the Gnostic view of the Christian mystic Jakob (*yah*-kawp) Böhme (*ber*-muh) [1575-1624], "a 'high deep blue' mixed with green signifies 'Liberty,' that is, the inner 'Kingdom of Glory' of the reborn soul." See Jung, *The Archetypes and the Collective Unconscious* 313. *In the Line of Melchizedek*

then scans his sheet: The Hermetic artist seeks at once "to analyze (verse)"; "to look at closely or in a broad, searching way" its "printed characters"; and "to examine, identify, or interpret" the Word of God ("Scan" [vt.], defs. 1, 2, 4). The *sheet* that he inspects is Holy Scripture. *The Round Chaos*

then self-excited bide / In mystic Oneness: Ultimately, the believer-priest negotiates the mystery of the universe through spiritual union with Christ. Cf. Davies, *The Mind of God* 231: "We cannot know" any Absolute "by rational means, for any Absolute, being a Unity and hence complete within itself, must include itself." *The Set-Up*

Then stands upon the globe by God's decree: Cf. Jung, *Psychology and Alchemy* 324, fig. 164, where Mercurius *stands* on the round chaos, the "confused assortment of crude disordered matter" (144n59) that, containing all the elements, not only prefigures the gold, but also gives birth to the *lapis philosophorum*—the living philosophical stone (325). *Inmate of Space*

They tease their waxen selves: The speaker alludes to wild honey bees that "convert the sugar contents of honey into wax, which oozes through the bees' small pores to produce tiny flakes of wax on their abdomens. Workers chew [or *tease*, i.e., separate] these pieces of wax until they become soft and moldable, and then add the chewed wax to the honeycomb construction." (See "How Do Honey Bees Make Hives?," advertisement, *Orkin* 16 Aug. 2014 <http://www.orkin.com/stinging-pests/bees/how-do-honeybees-make-hives/>.) *An Image of an Image*

This blessed greenness: "the alchemical *benedicta viriditas*, the blessed greenness, signifying on the one hand the 'leprosy of the metals' (verdigris), but on the other the secret immanence of the divine spirit of life in all things" (Jung, *Mysterium Coniunctionis* 432). *Crystal*

This nature that conquers the natures: a description of the redemptive character of alchemy. Although the speaker may be fixated at first on the material substances of the hermetic art, he ultimately seeks the salvation of the immortal inner man through the spiritual regeneration of matter. Cf. "the mystic logion" of the Greek-Egyptian alchemist Zosimos (c. AD 300) cited in *Psychology and Alchemy* 386: "And what meaneth this: 'the nature that conquers the natures,' and 'it [the transforming substance] is perfected and becometh like a whirl'?"—i.e., like "the revolving heavens [. . .] reflected in the unconscious." In other words, for the alchemists, "'nature' can improve or free itself from error only in and through itself" (*Aion* 143). *The End of Ourselves*

The three times the four: a reference to "the axiom of Maria" (a legendary Hebrew prophetess also known as the sister of Moses)—"'One becomes two, two becomes three, and out of the third comes the One as the fourth'" (Jung, *Psychology and Alchemy* 160). However, Jung observes that, in alchemical literature, since "Four signifies the feminine, motherly, [and] physical," while three represents "the masculine, fatherly, [and] spiritual [. . .], the uncertainty as to three or four" often amounts, in any definition of the holistic self, "to a wavering between the spiritual and the physical—a striking example of how every human truth is a last truth but one" (26-27). In fact, "Even in the axiom of Maria Prophetissa the quaternity is muffled and alembicated" (26). (For Jung's analysis of the number 12 itself—i.e., "four times three"—as a *reconfiguration* of the axiom of Maria, see the note above on "Maria's twelves.") *The End of Ourselves*

thrust from Flatland: an image that evokes the two-dimensional world of *Flatland: A Romance of Many Dimensions*, a satirical novella written by Edwin Abbott Abbott and first published in 1884. If he were pushed *from Flatland* into a three-dimensional world, the hyphenated coheir of Christ might soon find himself adrift in the fourth dimension. *A Cloud in Slow Motion*

Thumb like a gum, the resin of the few: With a phallic quip, the speaker celebrates *gum* arabic—in alchemy, not just "a synonym for the [adhesive] transforming substance," but also an emblem of "the androgynous original man of Gnosticism" (Jung, *Psychology and Alchemy* 161). *Tattoo*

Till all of the souls shall have left his sight: Cf. Jung, *Mysterium Coniunctionis* 413-14: For the Cabalists, the first-created Adam "appears on the one hand as the body of the people of Israel and on the other as its 'general soul.' [. . .] As the inner man, however, he is the totality of the individual, the synthesis of all parts of the psyche, and therefore of the conscious and the unconscious." Thus, from a Jungian perspective, "The 'going out' of the souls from the Primordial Man can be understood as the projection of a psychic integration process: The saving wholeness of the inner man—i.e., the 'Messiah'—cannot come about until all parts of the psyche have been made conscious." *Crystal*

Till I spanned the square as round as belief: The speaker surveys Calvary from the perspective of the Cross. The *square* is at once Golgotha, the Cross, and the quaternary speaker himself. The line also yields a veiled metaphor, the squaring of the circle, defined by Jung as "a stage on the way to the unconscious, a point of transition leading to a goal lying as yet unformulated beyond it." To ascertain the speaker's "goal," see *Psychology and Alchemy* 125-27, especially fig. 60, where the artifex squares the circle in order "to make the two sexes one whole." *Spacetime's Handkerchief*

Till Our Savior curved, His hourglass mated: According to Jung, the androgynous Christ—characterized here by the curvaceous bulbs of the hourglass—"is perhaps the most highly developed and differentiated symbol of the self, apart from the figure of the Buddha" (*Psychology and Alchemy* 19). *Servant of Nature*

To become ourselves we become concrete: In *The Sickness unto Death*, Kierkegaard maintains that "To become oneself [. . .] is to become something concrete. But to become something concrete is neither to become finite nor to become infinite, for that which is to become concrete is indeed a synthesis [of finitude and infinitude]" (59). In other words, in each individual searcher conscious of having an eternal self, "this [hyphenated] self takes on a new quality and specification [. . .]. This self is no longer the merely human self"; rather, it is "the theological self, the self directly before God. [. . .] But what an infinite accent is laid upon the self when it acquires God as its standard! The standard for the self is always: that directly in the face of which it is a self" (111). *The Round Chaos*

To calculate the lie thus eased the guy: Here, *the lie* signifies both the lay of the land (Golgotha or Skull Place) and the speaker's self-serving fiction concerning his cosmic identity, while *the guy*—another pun—means "a rope, chain, or rod attached to something to steady or guide it" ("Guy¹"[n.], def.), as well as "a man," or a "fellow," or "any person" ("Guy²" [n.], def. 3). In short, as Christ's coheir, the speaker attempts not just to "comfort" the crucifer (his archetypal alter ego), but also to "reduce the strain, tension, or pressure" of his cross ("Ease" [vt.], defs. 1, 4). *Eros' Meal*

***To consummate His sigh appeased the tie*:** To duplicate the life of Christ on Earth, the speaker tries "to pacify or quiet, especially by giving in to the demands of," the Savior's Cross ("Appease" [vt.], def. 1). The term *consummate* suggests, paradoxically, that the speaker can fulfill his goal only if he sublimates his eros. Cf. John 19.30: "'It is accomplished.'" *Eros' Meal*

***A torso like a seat, it has a cleat*:** The Lower Torso Assembly of NASA's Shuttle spacesuit is designed to cover the astronaut's legs and feet. However, during spacewalks, the astronaut wears an outer boot with "a rigid sole" and a fitted "heel clip" that can lock into foot restraints on the exterior of the International Space Station (ISS) and "on the robotic arm." See Stuart Morgan, "Footwear in the extreme environment of space," *SATRA Bulletin* May 2010, *SATRA Technology* 1 Nov. 2014 <http://www.satra.co.uk/bulletin/article_view.php?id=463>. In addition, see *Functional Clothing Design: From Sportswear to Spacesuits* (1995; New York: Fairchild Books-Bloomsbury, 2015) 343-44, where Susan M. Watkins and Lucy E. Dunne note that "A number of different features were used to help the astronauts stand in place at a workstation." Thus, "Some shoes had triangular cleats that matched a gridding in the floor of the station. These [cleats] were raised slightly off the surface of the shoe sole. When an astronaut wished to stay in one location, he would push the sole cleat through the floor grid and give it a quarter turn, so that the points of the cleats locked under the sides of the triangles in the floor grid." In fact, "A mushroom-shaped cleat that could be slipped in and out of the grid more easily was also used. . . . Many other ways of holding shoes in place on the floor of a space vehicle have been attempted—from magnetic cleats to suction cups." *Tattoo*

***A torso like a sheet, it has a pleat*:** Modular in design, the Space Shuttle's Extravehicular Mobility Unit, or EMU, "has 13 layers of material, including an inner cooling garment (two layers), [a] pressure garment (two layers), [a] thermal micrometeoroid garment (eight layers), and [an] outer cover (one layer). [. . .] All of the layers are sewn and cemented together [like a sheet of skin] to form the suit. In contrast to early space suits, which were individually tailored for each astronaut, the EMU has component pieces of varying sizes that can be put together to fit any given astronaut" (Craig Freudenrich, "How Space Suits Work" 18 Nov. 2014 <http://science.howstuffworks.com/space-suit4.htm>). In this poem, the speaker notes that, among its several features, the two-piece EMU spacesuit also provides *a pleat*, i.e., "a polyester structural restraint layer with folded and pleated joints," for mobility. (See "Space Educators' Handbook: The Spacesuit" 10 Nov. 2014 <http://er.jsc.nasa.gov/seh/suitnasa.html>.) *Tattoo*

torus: the universe pictured as a hyperdoughnut, one of the "strange topologies" that Michio Kaku predicates in *Hyperspace* 94-98. *Living in Curved Space*

***Tossed veronica, courtship's la-di-da*:** Here, the handkerchief with which Saint Veronica wiped the face of Jesus on the way to Calvary becomes the cherished token flung to a lover as a form of either pretentious or "affected [. . .] behavior" ("La-di-da" [n.], def. 2). *Orpheus' Rite*

Transmitted like an atom tipped the case: The speaker suggests that he fell through the hole left in space by a collapsing star, i.e., a black hole, "a vestige of vanished matter—a violently distorted region" from which nothing escapes, not even light (Davies, *Other Worlds* 168). In *Space-Time and Beyond*, Toben, "in conversation" with Sarfatti and Wolf, further elucidates this phenomenon: "To understand time travel, we must look at space-time itself. In the ordinary picture used by most physicists, space-time is flat. This means that each point of space-time has its own light cone [i.e., a wall of light that separates a given reality from other realities] and that the light cones of different points are parallel to each other. However, the situation changes when rotating black holes appear within space. Some of the light cones are now tipped over by the gravitational field, forming 'closed timelike curves' (called time machines by [the physicist] Brandon Carter). This means that one can follow a path through the inner of the two event horizons [. . .]"—in effect, beyond eternity, through the trapped region inside the blackhole. Thus, "The path avoids hitting the timelike ring singularity of the rotating blackhole," a trajectory "which allows time-travel into another universe, or even into one's own past" (133). *Trismegistus' Art*

Triassic: a geologic period of the Mesozoic Era (245-208 million years ago) characterized by the appearance of the first dinosaurs. *Bio*

trilobites (try-low-bytes): marine arthropods; invertebrate animals with jointed legs and segmented bodies—e.g., insects, crustaceans, and arachnids—found as fossils in Paleozoic rocks. *Bio*

The true star in him: According to Paracelsus, the Swiss physician and alchemist (1493-1541), the *filius philosophorum* [the son of the philosophers] could be "extracted from matter by human art and, by means of the opus, made into a new light-bringer" (Jung, *Alchemical Studies* 127). *The Crowned Hermaphrodite*

Turns like a city in this band of lines: The speaker, eros-propelled, is compared to the City of God. The *band of lines* refers to Mars and Venus, lovers not merely "caught in the net of Vulcan," but also "imprisoned in the embrace of Physis [i.e., Nature, or the phenomenal world]" (Jung, *Psychology and Alchemy* 202, 401). *Living in Curved Space*

Twin phantoms [. . .] / Scattered Alice: In *Alice in Quantumland*, Gilmore imagines that the anti-*Alice* particle had traveled along "until it collided with an Alice [particle]," the latter going backward in time, and that "the two mutually annihilated one another" (100). *The Quantum Alice*

Undivided point: a Gnostic God-image, "the 'grain of mustard seed' that grows into the kingdom of God" and that, like a *point*, "is 'present in the body'" (Jung, *Aion* 198). *Hourglass*

unit, ghost, or probe: From the speaker's standpoint, the distant trace of

Canopus might be either an astronaut attached to his Manned Maneuvering Unit (MMU), a spirit like a breath-soul, or an unmanned "instrumented spacecraft" ("Probe" [n.], def. 4). *Eros' Meal*

unit glassed: the MMU (Manned Maneuvering Unit), a now-defunct propulsion device, couched here as a metonymy for the helmeted (and hence glass-encased) astronaut. The phrase evokes the image of the astronaut as a wandering microcosm. See also Jung's assessment of the Monad (the indivisible point), conceived by the Gnostics as an emblem of "perfect Man" (*Aion* 218-19). *Citizen of the Cosmos*

Unit maneuvering at the throttle: the modern astronaut cast by Mother Earth as both an archetype of the Original Man and an ideal human. In this context, the term *Unit* denotes, as an appositive, "a single person [. . .], especially as distinguished from others" ("Unit" [n.], def. 3a), and connotes, as both appositive and synecdoche, the Shuttle's peculiar module, the Manned Maneuvering Unit (MMU)—seemingly "a backpack with armrests"—that "has enabled astronauts, for the first time, to orbit for brief periods without any umbilical line or safety tether [attached] to their spaceships" (Allen and Martin, *Entering Space* 113). *The Power of Life*

Unit wound in the void: either the incarnate Christ or the tethered astronaut—His coheir—suspended in the vacuum of space. *Tabernacled*

Unseen from the womb, unshod and unarmed: Cf. Plato's description of primordial man as a species "'naked, unshod, unbedded, and unarmed'" in "Protagoras," sections 320d-321e (qtd. in Zajonc, *Catching the Light* 10). *Entwining the Light*

Until the foam unfurls and then a froth: In *Other Worlds*, Davies argues that ripples and waves in the fabric of Spacetime—what he calls the local gravitation fields—"become so distorted that they break up into foam. The apparently smooth unbroken surface [of Spacetime] is really a seething mass of tiny spume and bubbles [. . .]" (96). *Citizen of the Cosmos*

upon His wain: In her role not only as Sophia, the matrix of feminine Wisdom, but also as Co-Redemptrix, the Blessed Virgin Mary accompanies Jesus to Golgotha on a large, open farm wagon, an emblem of their lowly social status. *Living in Curved Space*

Upraised the Host: See Matt. 26.26-28: At the Last Supper, "Jesus took bread, and having said the blessing he broke it and gave it to the disciples with the words: 'Take this and eat; this is my body.' Then he took a cup, and having offered thanks to God he gave it to them with the words, 'Drink from it, all of you. For this is my blood, the blood of the covenant, shed for many for the forgiveness of sins.'" (Jesus also shares the paschal meal with His apostles in Mark 14.22-25.) *An Image of an Image*

Urged their vital parts around to the front: See J. Bronowski, *The Ascent of Man* (Boston: Little, Brown, 1973) 401: "We are the only species that copulates face to face, and this is universal in all cultures. To my mind, it is an expression of a general equality which has been important in the evolution of man, I think, right back to the time of *Australopithecus* and the first tool-makers." *Tattoo*

Vega passing, Arcturus like a crust: In June, when the sun reaches the solstice, "Arcturus [in the constellation Boötes] dominates the western sky while Vega in *Lyra* [. . .] passes overhead" (Engelbrektson, *Stars, Planets, and Galaxies* 42). See also Patrick Moore, *Travellers in Space and Time* (New York: Doubleday, 1984) 92: "Arcturus is a powerful star. Yet on Earth, at a range of 36 light-years, we can detect almost no heat from it." It seems but *a crust*, a piece of ice-cold earth, and nothing more. *The Foliate Pebble*

Verdigris (ver-duh-*grease*) essential: an elliptical nominative absolute (*Verdigris* [being] *essential*); the green or greenish-blue rust that forms on brass, bronze, or copper. "In the alchemical view, rust, like verdigris, is the metal's sickness. But at the same time this leprosy is [. . .] the basis for the preparation of the philosophical gold." In other words, "there is no light without shadow and no psychic wholeness without imperfection," a paradox that Jung examines in *Psychology and Alchemy* 159. *Elapid's Cowl*

Vestibular pathways adjust the sky: The speaker imagines that, like Heracles (or Hercules)—here, a stand-in for the giant deity Atlas—he hefts the vault of the *sky*. The phrase *Vestibular pathways* refers to the membranous labyrinth, the space in the inner ear that includes two sacs with "systems of receptor cells and calcium crystals that respond to gravitational and accelerating forces and so relay information concerning the position of the head. Thus, in addition to the organ of hearing, the inner ear [. . .] contains the balancing organs," also called vestibular organs, "because of their location in the vestibule," the cavity that leads into the cochlea (Nilsson and Lindberg, *Behold Man* 211). *Spinner*

vine like a tree: In Babylonian literature, Ishtar, "The Lady of the vine stalk [who] languishes" for Tammuz, her dead son, anticipates the Blessed Mother, who grieves for Christ (Baring and Cashford, *Myth of the Goddess* 222). See also Jung, *Psychology and Alchemy*, fig. 231, where "the tree is shown as a naked virgin wearing a crown" (419-20). *Eros' Meal*

vitrified his meat: The mercurial speaker felt that he had become a pneumatic body: "a breath-body or subtle body not subject to corruption" (Jung, *Symbols of Transformation* 332). *Trismegistus' Art*

Void like the adder: both the cosmic singularity projected as a serpentine point and the totalistic "symbol of the uroboros, the snake that bites its own tail" (Jung, *Aion* 190). *Citizen of the Cosmos*

The void that but the vacuum rations: In *Perfect Symmetry: The Search for the Beginning of Time* (New York: Simon, 1985), Heinz R. Pagels remarks that, according to the 1984 Stephen Hawking-James Hartle model of the origin of the universe, "The nothingness 'before' the creation of the universe is the most complete void that we can imagine—no space, time or matter existed. It is a world without place, without duration or eternity, without number—it is what the mathematicians call 'the empty set.' Yet this unthinkable void converts itself into the plenum of existence—a necessary consequence of physical laws" (347). *The Power of Life*

wain: a cart or a large, open farm wagon—here, an emblem of lowly social status. *Living in Curved Space*

waters composite: in alchemy, "the philosophical water [that] is the stone [a symbol of the miraculously transformed adept] or the *prima materia* itself [. . .]" (Jung, *Psychology and Alchemy* 235, 269-70). *The Set-Up*

a water shed He: Cf. John 19.34: After the death of Jesus on the Cross, "one of the soldiers stabbed his side with a lance, and at once there was a flow of blood and water." The term "watershed" denotes, of course, a critical dividing point or line, as Jung, highlighting the etymology of the German *Wasserscheide* ("watershed") and *Scheide* ("vagina"), recognizes—with a difference—in *Symbols of Transformation*: "Where the roads *cross* and enter into one another, thereby symbolizing the union of opposites, there is the 'mother,' the object and epitome of all union. Where the roads *divide*, where there is parting, separation, splitting, there we find the 'division,' the cleft—the symbol of the mother and at the same time the essence of what the mother means for us, namely cleavage and farewell" (64). See also Jesus' declaration in Mark 3.35: "'Who is my mother? [. . .] Whoever does the will of God is [. . .] my mother.'" *Citizen of the Cosmos*

wave on the shore / That streaks like a web: a roller—a heavy, swelling wave—that breaks, or is about to break, into foam upon the shoreline even as it weaves like the filmy network of either a spider (e.g., the Bowl and Doily Spider) or a spiral galaxy. *A Cloud in Slow Motion*

Wave's interference, insight infinite: In *Other Worlds*, Davies explains that electrons, if liberated, "will spill out in many directions, spreading about like the ripples on a pond" (63). However, in the two-slit experiment, "The interference that occurs [. . .] cannot be between many different electrons, or the pattern would disappear when only one electron at a time is used. It is an interference of probability," i.e., of probability waves (67). In other words, for each electron, both slits "must be left open; either [slit] offers a potential path, though only one can be the actual path. Which one we can never know" (69). *The Quantum Alice*

a wavier Savior pursed: either the quantum Christ described by a specific wavefunction (i.e., here, by the units of information encoded in an isolated system of multiple particles) or the consecrated Communion wafer carried in a pyx, the latter container itself placed in a leather purse. *Navel*

We are without excuse things that are made: Cf. Saint Bonaventure's thesis, underscored in *The Soul's Journey into God*, that "*from the creation of the world / the* *invisible attributes of God are clearly seen, / being understood / through the things that are made.* / And so those who do not wish to heed these things, / and to know, bless and love / God / in all of them / *are without excuse;* / for they are unwilling to be transported / *out of darkness / into the marvelous light* of God" (*The Soul's Journey into God, The Tree of Life, The Life of St. Francis*, trans. Ewert Cousins [New Jersey: Paulist Press, 1978] 77). See also Rom. 1.19-21: "For all that may be known of God by men lies plain before their eyes; indeed God himself has disclosed it to them. His invisible attributes, that is to say his everlasting power and deity, have been made visible, ever since the world began, to the eye of reason, in the things that he has made. There is [. . .] no possible defence for their conduct; knowing God, they have refused to honour him as God, or to render him thanks." *Eros' Meal*

Web like the whirlwind: the Milky Way Galaxy viewed as a gigantic spiral wheel or even as the veil of the cosmic illusionist Maya. *Citizen of the Cosmos*

We have trampled on the garment of shame: See "the fragment from the Gospel according to the Egyptians cited by [the Greek Christian theologian] Clement of Alexandria" (c. 150–c. 215) and quoted by Jung in *Mysterium Coniunctionis* 374: "'When ye have trampled on the garment of shame, and when the two become one and the male with the female is neither male nor female.'" *Courtship*

***we pass through a slit*:** The speaker alludes not only to the two-*slit* experiment that validated the quantum concept of wave-particle duality, but also to the arduous passage, through the walls of the uterus, and out of the vagina, of a full-term foetus. *The Quantum Alice*

***We roll the ball as into a sinter*:** Fantasizing, we move or turn the cosmic fireball, over and over, playfully, in the palm of the hand, even as we might shift a still-burning coal. *Cinderdust*

We try each door that the Hubble unlocked: In "When Galaxies Collide," Begley ponders "all the secrets that the Hubble [Space Telescope] has unlocked," especially "its images of galaxies that formed when the universe was in its infancy" (5). *Courtship*

What myrtle in the arbor regnant hints: See Jung, *Symbols of Transformation* 219: "Numerous myths say that human beings came from trees, and many of them tell how the hero was enclosed in the maternal tree-trunk, like [. . .] Adonis in the myrtle [. . .]." Although such myths suggest an "incest tendency," Jung emphasizes that "the basis of the 'incestuous' desire is not cohabitation, but, as every sun myth shows, the strange idea of becoming a child again, of returning to the parental shelter, and of entering into the mother in order to be reborn through her" (223-24). *The Set-Up*

wheel like a king's: the Sun conceived as an archetypal expression of the Heavenly King. See Chevalier and Gheerbrant, *The Penguin Dictionary of Symbols* 1099: In the majority of cultures, the *wheel* "is a solar symbol," even as the Sun itself is either a god or "a manifestation of the godhead" (945). *Split-Minded*

When Jesus died, they dressed Him like a tot; / Swathed His cadaver; sealed Him in a grot: Cf. John 19.40-42: After Jesus' death, Joseph of Arimathaea and Nicodemus "took the body of Jesus and wrapped it, with the spices [myrrh and aloes], in strips of linen cloth according to Jewish burial-customs. Now, at the place where he had been crucified there was a garden, and in the garden a new tomb, not yet used for burial. There, because the tomb was near at hand and it was the eve of the Jewish Sabbath, they laid Jesus." In *Jesus: The Evidence*, Wilson adds that "The nineteenth-century edicule [or 'little building'] within the [restored] Church of the Holy Sepulchre"—the latter edifice at one time located outside Jerusalem's walls—enshrines "what remains of the reputed tomb of Jesus" (140). *God's Folly*

When old stars in globular clusters merge, / Out of their ashes protoplanets surge: Cf. Begley, "When Galaxies Collide" 4: "In the ultimate heavenly recycling, old stars in globular clusters merge, and out of their ashes [or gas] a new star is born. Contrary to the textbooks, globular clusters do not contain only old stars." See also "Planets in Globular Clusters?," where Steinn Sigurdsson suggests that "planetary systems may be detected around the recycled pulsars found in globular clusters" (*The Astrophysical Journal* 399.1: L95-L97, 1 Nov. 1992, *The Smithsonian/NASA Astrophysics Data System* 5 Dec. 2014 <http://articles.adsabs.harvard.edu/full/gif/1992Apj...399L...955/L000095.000.html>). *Courtship*

when streaked by light I sprint, / Like metal glint: The speaker compares the Christian athlete of 1 Cor. 9.24-25 to Hermes, the Greek god of revelation who also served as messenger, scribe and herald for the other gods; to the alchemical Mercurius or Mercury (the Roman counterpart of Hermes), "the world-creating spirit concealed in matter" (Jung, *Psychology and Alchemy* 293); and—in a benign reincarnation—even to the liquid metal man, the quicksilver trickster of the James Cameron film *Terminator 2: Judgment Day* (1991). Equally pertinent, throughout this poem, is the mandate from 1 Tim. 6.12: "Run the great race of faith and take hold of eternal life." *Liquid Metal Man*

Whereas the toad submersed in solid earth / Awaits its house: In *Mysterium Coniunctionis*, Jung explains that, according to the alchemist Michael Maier [1568-1622], the *toad*, a terrestrial amphibian, "'denotes the philosophic earth, which cannot fly [i.e., cannot be sublimated],'" since, unlike air, "'it is firm and solid. Upon it as a foundation the golden house is to be built'" (4). In this context, the golden *house* is, of course, a symbol of the holistic self. *Astronaut*

whether clay or pottle: whether "firm, fine-grained earth" ("Clay" [n.], def. 1a) or "a pot or tankard" of wine ("Pottle" [n.], def. 2). Here, the phrase also carries the hidden metaphor of the Eucharist. *The Power of Life*

whether now or then: The speaker suggests that one's perception of Spacetime is delayed rather than immediate. In other words, as Harth speculates in *Windows on the Mind*, "A conscious response to a stimulus cannot occur [. . .] unless some form of neuronal reverberation continues for up to about half a second, the *adequate* time for sensation. On the other hand, *when* sensation sets in, the subjective judgment of its timing *refers* it back close to the time when the actual event took place. It appears that sensations are replays of events that are well in the past, but manage to convey to us the delusion of a conscious immediacy and participation" (201-02). In effect, "The brain is the epitome of a self-referent system. My self is forever imaging itself and changing in response to the image. It can never quite catch up with itself" (215). *God's Folly*

White as solid snow He flies in the storm: "what the alchemists had in mind when they spoke of [the philosophic] Mercurius" as an analogue of the Holy Spirit—quicksilver, "but a very special kind of quicksilver": a life force "'who flies like solid white snow'" (Jung, *Alchemical Studies* 211, 214). Jung attributes the latter epithet to Nicholaus Niger Happelius, "Aphorismi Basiliani," *Theatrum chemicum*, vol. 4 (1613; Strasbourg: Argentorati, 1659) 327. *Apostolates*

wintered: In virtual reality, after her atomic collision, Alice has seemingly passed or spent "the coldest season of the year" in an atmosphere marked either by "decline, dreariness, [and] adversity" ("Winter" [vi.], def. 1; [n.], defs. 3, 1a) or —characteristic of nuclear winter—by a blanket of smoke, ashen darkness, and frigid temperatures. *The Quantum Alice*

Without a father he could not exist: The pronoun refers either to Christ or to the speaker. Thus, the heavenly *father* is—for both Christ and His coheir—Yahweh; Christ's designated earthly *father* is, of course, Saint Joseph. See also Paul's description of Melchizedek, king of Salem, in Heb. 7.3: "He has no father, no mother, no lineage; his years have no beginning, his life no end. He is like the Son of God: he remains a priest for all time." *The Power of Life*

Without a mother—side lanced like a cyst: Christ's heavenly *mother* (Mary), like the speaker's earthly *mother* (Evelyn), had delivered her son to the world of instinct. In the iconography of the medieval Church, Christ is often shown as a unicorn slain in the Virgin's lap, a canny pietà that portrays Mary as both hunter and pacifier (Jung, *Psychology and Alchemy* 438-39, figs. 241 and 242). See also the picture of Melusina, the crowned water-nymph who pierces Christ's *side* with a lance—a woodprint from Hieronymus Reusner's *Pandora* (1588)—in Jung, *Alchemical Studies* B4. *The Power of Life*

Without offense: In *The Sickness unto Death*, Kierkegaard suggests that, as a sinner, the individual "is separated from God by the most yawning qualitative abyss" and that "God is separated [...] from man in turn by the same yawning qualitative abyss when he forgives sins" (155). Accordingly, from His bema-seat in Heaven, God *looks down*. Yet, strangely enough, through His unbridgeable distance, He empowers Christianity. Indeed, this *is* Christianity: "with this [stipulation] Christianity begins." It says to each particular human being: "either you shall be offended [because you shall be judged by the infinite Redeemer], or you shall believe. Not one word more; there is nothing more to add" (155-56). Of course, as Kierkegaard indicates elsewhere, "to be offended is sin" (150n). *The Cheshire of Sense; A Cloud in Slow Motion*

With rivets of love: See Zajonc, *Catching the Light* 20: According to the philosopher and poet Empedocles [5th cent. BC], "the divine Aphrodite, goddess of love, fashioned our eyes out of the four Greek elements of earth, water, air, and fire, fitting them together with rivets [i.e., metal pins or bolts] of love." *Entwining the Light*

With this *left over, as the Lord has said*: the multiplying loaves and fishes given by Christ to His followers: "They all ate to their hearts' content; and the scraps left over, which they picked up, were enough to fill twelve great baskets" (Matt. 14.20). *Elapid's Cowl*

wolds: "treeless, rolling plains," especially high ones ("Wold¹" [n.], def.). *In the Line of Melchizedek*

woman like a mentor: The simile melds a specific woman with a universal form or archetype—namely, "the feminine side of the male psyche": the anima. Both companions would spur the riven Adam to such "consummate selfhood" as Jungian psychologists call "the realization of a completely individuated and integrated personality" (Calvin S. Hall and Vernon J. Nordby, *A Primer of Jungian Psychology* [New York: Mentor-New American, 1973] 46, 82, 85). In this regard, Hall and Nordby summarize Jung's position trenchantly: "The man who has integrated his anima with his maleness is *not* one whose behavior is sometimes in the masculine mode and sometimes in the feminine mode. He is *not* part man and part woman. Rather, a true synthesis between opposites has been achieved so that it may be said [that] transcendence [a unifying function inherent in the individual] has abolished gender except in a biological sense" (85). *Spacetime's Handkerchief*

wool aubergine: an allusion to the dark purple fleece of the Sacrificial Lamb. *In the Line of Melchizedek*

The world evolved as from a ghostly point: The image evokes a checkered cosmogonic myth: The universe sprang from both the big-bang singularity and the mind of the Original (hermaphroditic) Man, the undivided *point* "present in the body" (Jung, *Aion* 198-99). *God's Folly*

The world is like a string: In *The Whole Shebang*, Ferris states that, according to superstring theories, "subatomic particles are actually tiny strings made of space. [. . .] Strings are so small that when viewed from a distance—meaning at any wavelength of light or any other form of electromagnetic illumination—they 'look like' infinitesimal particles" (220). *Living in Curved Space*

The world that we know is passing away: Cf. 1 Cor. 7.29, 31: "The time we live in will not last long. [. . .] For the whole frame of this world is passing away." *Inmate of Space*

wound in the cast: wrapped in the elaborate shroud of the mummified centuries. The metaphor is also theatrical—Christ leads, even as He indwells, His coheirs in the paschal drama of salvation. *Citizen of the Cosmos*

Wound me in chaos like Adam, Eve's slave, / Joseph in the cistern, Christ in His cave: See Jung, *Psychology and Alchemy* 333, fig. 170. All three heroes—*Adam, Joseph,* and *Christ*—undertake the night sea journey, "a descent into the dark world of the unconscious [. . .] whose end and aim is the restoration of life, resurrection, and the triumph over death [. . .]" (329). *A Cloud in Slow Motion*

Wrapped in gossamer, [. . .] / tether hooks that curl: a description of the astronaut's multi-layered spacesuit. The verbal portrait here mirrors the photograph of astronaut Bob Stewart in Allen and Martin, *Entering Space* 112. Stewart "is attached to the manned maneuvering unit," a jet-propelled "backpack with armrests," a kind of "rocket chair" that enables the astronaut to fly untethered in space. "Near his right elbow are tether hooks to which a variety of objects can be secured" (113). Clearly, in the poem, the astronaut is not unlike the primordial figures of the *anima mundi* and the Original Man—in short, a God-image latent in the darkness of matter that, "because of its quaternary character and its roundness, must be regarded as a symbol of wholeness." See Jung, *Aion* 198. *Astronaut*

Wry in his make: The model human, still evolving, is "turned or bent to one side"; "stubbornly contrary"; "distorted in meaning"; "perverse" and/or "ironic" ("Wry" [adj.], defs. 1, 3, 4, 5). To visualize the astronaut's "wry" stance, see the iconic photograph of Bruce McCandless, in Allen and Martin, *Entering Space* 110-11: His body atilt, McCandless operates the MMU (the Manned Maneuvering Unit). *The Power of Life*

Yahweh (yah-way): "God: a form [i.e., a modern reconstruction] of the Hebrew name in the Old Testament [. . .]" ("Yahweh" [n.], def.). *Orpheus' Rite*

Yahweh's Cheshire grinning: Cosmos, star, planet, species, the individual speaker himself—all shall, like the *Cheshire* cat in Lewis Carroll's *Alice's Adventures in Wonderland*, wink out. *Cinderdust*

yod: not only the tenth letter of the Hebrew alphabet, but also the Gnostic symbol of the indivisible point, i.e., of the "perfect and indivisible man." Thus, "The Original Man, Adam, signifies the small hook at the top of the letter Yod" (Jung, *Aion* 218n136). The word rhymes with "wood." *Trismegistus' Art*

Zion: Mount *Zion*, the site of "that new Jerusalem which is coming down out of heaven [. . .]" (Rev. 3.12) at End-time. *Finite Infinite; Tabernacled*

www.ingramcontent.com/pod-product-compliance
Lightning Source LLC
Chambersburg PA
CBHW081349080526
44588CB00016B/2429